TAKE BACK YOUR LIFE

A 40-DAY INTERACTIVE JOURNEY TO
THINKING RIGHT SO YOU CAN LIVE RIGHT

STUDY GUIDE | FIVE SESSIONS

LEVI LUSKO

W PUBLISHING GROUP

AN IMPRINT OF THOMAS NELSON

CONTENTS

INTRODUCTION

There's a great story told in the each of the Gospels about a certain event that involved Jesus, the twelve disciples, a few loaves of bread and some fish, and about 5,000 people. It had been a long day, especially for Jesus. He had awoken to the news that his cousin John the Baptist had been put to death at the hands of the mad King Herod. The news had sent him into a personal retreat. But the crowds had followed him to that remote place, and Jesus—feeling compassion for them—had ministered to them and healed their sick.

Now, as that long day was drawing to an end, the disciples were feeling a bit edgy. It was late, and the people needed to go home in time to get to the villages and buy food for dinner. It was then that Jesus gave them a little assignment: "You give them something to eat" (Matthew 14:16). The disciples quickly calculated "that would take more than half a year's wages" (Mark 6:37). Andrew was able to dig up five barley loaves and two fish from a boy with a lunch, but he added, "how far will they go amoung so many?" (John 6:9).

Jesus replied to each of these concerns by having the disciples sit the people "in groups of about fifty each" (Luke 9:14). He took the loaves and fish, gave thanks for them, and then had the disciples start handing them out . . . and everyone was fed. Jesus then had his disciples gather up the excess food. As a result, the disciples had twelve full baskets to take with them as they sailed through a storm on the Sea of Galilee.

In the same way, I've combed through my sermons and notes from when I was writing two previous books and gathered up the best of the leftovers for you to take on your stormy seas. Instead of being collected in twelve baskets, this journey is broken up into forty days. Why forty? Well, life supposedly begins at forty. It sure did for Moses—the guy we will discuss in our first session—who spent the first forty years of his life thinking he was somebody, the second forty years of his life finding out he was nobody, and the final forty years of his life discovering what God can do with somebody who knows he is a nobody.

The number forty comes up throughout Scripture again and again. In Noah's day, rain fell for forty days and forty nights (see Genesis 7:4). The spies sent by Moses to explore the promised land did so for forty days (see Numbers 13:25). The Israelites after the generation of the exodus wandered in the wilderness for forty years (see Numbers 32:13). Goliath taunted the Israelites for forty days before David cut him down (see 1 Samuel 17:16). Jesus fasted forty days and forty nights in the desert (see Matthew 4:2). Forty days was the period from the resurrection to the ascension (see Acts 1:3). And through these forty days I believe God is going to do something significant deep inside your soul that will mark you forever.

So, are you willing to commit to this forty-day journey? Are you, like the disciples, willing to let go of your own agenda and fears and see what God can do with your faith?

Are you willing to wage the battle for your heart and mind? For as we will see as we launch into this journey, such a battle is taking place. And you must fight to *take back your life*.

— Levi Lusko

HOW TO USE THIS GUIDE

The *Take Back Your Life* video study is designed to be experienced in a setting such as a Bible study, Sunday school class, or any small-group gathering. Each session begins with a brief welcome section and opening questions to get you thinking about the topic. You will then watch a video with Levi Lusko and engage in small-group discussion. You will close each session with a time of reflection and prayer.

To get the most out of your group experience, keep the following points in mind. First, the real growth in this study will happen during your small-group time. This is where you will process the content of the teaching for the week, ask questions, and learn from others as you hear what God is doing in their lives. For this reason, it is important for you to be fully committed to the group and attend each session so you can build trust and rapport with the other members. If you choose to only go through the motions, or if you refrain from participating, there is a lesser chance you will find what you're looking for during this study.

Second, remember the goal of your small group is to serve as a place where people can share, learn about God, and build intimacy and friendship. For this reason, seek to make your group a safe place. This means being honest about your thoughts and feelings and listening carefully to everyone else's opinion. (If you are a group leader, there are additional instructions and resources in the back of the book for leading a productive discussion group.)

Third, resist the temptation to fix a problem someone might be having or to correct his or her theology, as that is not the purpose of your small-group time. Also, keep everything your group shares confidential. This will foster a rewarding sense of community in your group and create a place where people can heal, be challenged, and grow spiritually.

Following your group time, you can maximize the impact of this course by completing the between-sessions activities. You can complete these personal studies all in one sitting or follow the recommended course and do one each day of the week. If you are unable to finish (or even start) these studies, still attend the group study video session. You are still wanted and welcome at the group even if you don't have your "homework" done.

Keep in mind that the videos, discussion questions, and activities are simply meant to kick-start your imagination so you are not only open to what God wants you to hear but also how to apply it to your life. As Jesus promised, "Ask, and it will be given to you; seek and you will find; knock, and the door will be opened to you" (Luke 11:9).

So ask, seek, and knock . . . and then listen to what the Lord is saying to you about *taking back your life*.

LOOK IN THE MIRROR

Reality is merely an illusion, albeit a very persistent one.

Albert Einstein

WELCOME

Harry Houdini was one of the greatest escape artists the world has ever seen. One of the most famous tricks he loved to perform was to escape from jail cells across the world. Houdini would travel to a city and challenge the citizens to create a cell from which he could not escape. He would always free himself in record time, whether he was in handcuffs, or the cell was triple locked, or he had to scale a wall to escape.

Of course, Houdini had a lot tricks up his sleeve. He would ask to test the lock with the key and make an impression of it using a small box of wax that he kept in his palm. He would then hide the key in his hair or the heel of his slippers. Other times, he was able to have the key passed to him from a friend after reaching his hands through the bars to shake hands with the onlookers. If all else failed, he had a special lock pick made that he could hide in his belt.

However, as one story goes, there was one cell in a town in the British Isles that stumped the great illusionist. Houdini walked into the challenge with confidence. Once the jail was closed, he took off his coat and set to work with his key and lock pick. But there was something unusal about the lock. He worked for thirty minutes with no success. An hour passed, and still he was stuck behind the bars. After two hours had passed, an exhausted Houdini collapsed against the door in defeat . . . and it swung open.

The citizens of the town had played a trick on Houdini by not locking the cell in the first place! The solution was there in plain sight. It had only been locked in his mind.

Sometimes, we fall into the same trap. We fail to recognize the reality of our situation because what our eyes are telling us does not represent the whole story. We fail to see the solutions in plain sight or are blind to what is really taking place. In particular, as we will discuss in this first session, we fail to see that we are in an invisible war . . . and that the battlefield for the struggle is located in our own hearts and minds.

SHARE

If you or any of your group members are just getting to know one another, take a few minutes to introduce yourselves. Then, to kick things off, discuss one of the following questions:

* When is a time in your life that you failed to see the solution to a problem that ended up being right in front of you?

— *or* —

* When is a time in your life that you failed to see that you were walking into a crisis? What was the situation and what happened as a result?

READ

Invite someone to read aloud the following passage. Listen for fresh insights as you hear the verses being read, and then discuss the questions that follow.

The god of this age has blinded the minds of unbelievers, so that they cannot see the light of the gospel that displays the glory of Christ, who is the image of God. For what we preach is not ourselves, but Jesus Christ as Lord, and ourselves as your servants for Jesus' sake. For God, who said, "Let light shine out of darkness," made his light shine in our hearts to give us the light of the knowledge of God's glory displayed in the face of Christ. . . .

Therefore we do not lose heart. Though outwardly we are wasting away, yet inwardly we are being renewed day by day. For our light and momentary troubles are achieving for us an eternal glory that far outweighs them all. So we fix our eyes not on what is seen, but on what is unseen, since what is seen is temporary, but what is unseen is eternal (2 Corinthians 4:4–6, 16–18).

What is one insight that stands out to you from this passage?

What does the apostle Paul say about the two realms that exist in this world?

WATCH

Play the video segment for session one. As you and your group watch, use the following outline to record any thoughts or concepts that stand out to you.

NOTES

We cannot rely on what we see because our eyes do not tell us the whole story of what is happening in this world. There is also an invisible conflict raging in the spiritual realm.

What do we see when we look into the mirror? The Bible says we should see someone who is loved by God and created in his image. But that person is being opposed by an enemy who is seeking to defeat us from the inside out.

There are four movements in the story of Moses that reveal how these two realities play out. In movement #1, *the devil works in Pharaoh's heart to destroy God's people.*

Moses is raised in the household of the person who was trying to kill him. He is brought up by Egyptians, though he is actually a Hebrew.

Satan had a plan of destroying God's people, but he had bigger plan of destroying the Messiah, who would come as the "greater Moses" to save us from our sins.

In movement #2, *Moses visits his people and takes vengeance against an Egyptian.*

Moses realizes that God made him for a unique purpose. He starts to realize that he is a "genius."

We all have God-given abilities that make us a genius at something. The problem is we also experience a pull from the enemy that tries to hold us back from greatness.

In movement #3, *Moses goes on the run after killing the Egyptian.*

Moses makes the mistake of doing the right thing at the wrong time and in the wrong way. He ends up as a fugitive because he operated out of God's timing.

A blessing out of season can become a burden. What we thought would bring us happiness ends up bringing us difficulty and complexity.

In movement #4, *Moses ultimately walks in God's calling for his life.*

After forty years, God appears to Moses in the desert and resissues the call on his life.

Moses, with God's power in his life, is able to tap into his inner genius and become a leader the likes of which the world has rarely seen.

As we fight through the battles we cannot see, we will we be able to do everything that God has called us to do.

DISCUSS

Take a few minutes with your group members to discuss what you just watched and explore these concepts together.

1. We are all involved in a spiritual war, and often the battlefield is our own hearts and minds. What are some of the ways these struggles play out in our lives?

2. Read aloud Ephesians 6:10–13. What strategies does Paul put forward in these verses on how to win the battles taking place in your heart and mind?

3. What do the movements in Moses' story reveal about stepping into God's plan for your life? How do you respond to the idea that you also have a special calling on your life?

4. What does Moses' story reveal about doing the right thing (following God's plan) in the right way and right time? When has what was intended to be a blessing in your life turned out to be a burden because you didn't follow God's timing?

5. What are some negative thoughts that have held you back in the past from stepping to God's call on your life or using your God-given abilities?

6. What are some practical steps you need to take today to *take back your life* when it comes to winning the war that is raging in your heart and mind?

RESPOND

Briefly review the outline for the video teaching and any notes you took. In the space below, write down the most significant point you took away from this session.

PRAY

Wrap up your time together by taking a few minutes to talk with God. Here are a few ideas of what you could pray about based on what you discussed in this session:

- Ask God to provide insights into ways the enemy is distorting your vision of his plan and clarity as to what God has called you to do.
- Pray for God's strength to overcome any fears that are holding you back.
- Thank God for his power to forgive sin in your life through the sacrifice of his Son, Jesus Christ, and for the gifts he has given you to use for his purposes.
- Declare that you will fix your eyes on God and follow his plan going forward.

BETWEEN-SESSIONS PERSONAL STUDY

You are involved in a war . . . and the battlefield is your mind. However, you are not defenseless in the fight. As Paul writes, you can "put on the full armor of God, so that you can take your stand against the devil's schemes" (Ephesians 6:11). A key part of putting on this armor involves immersing yourself in God's Word each day so his truths can reshape your thoughts. With this in mind, reflect on the material you covered this week by engaging in the following personal study. Each day offers a short reading adapted from *Take Back Your Life*, along with a few reflection questions to take you deeper into the theme of this week's study. (You may also want to revew week 1 of *Take Back Your Life* before you begin.) Be sure to read the reflection questions and make a few notes in your guide about the experience. At the start of the next session you will have a few minutes to share any insights you learned. But remember, the primary goal of these questions is for your own spiritual growth and private reflection.

HIDING IN PLAIN SIGHT

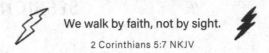

We walk by faith, not by sight.

2 Corinthians 5:7 NKJV

Looks can be deceiving. We can look at something but not see what's there. And that means we cannot trust what we see with the naked eye. This is how Paul put it: "So we fix our eyes not on what is seen, but on what is unseen, since what is seen is temporary, but what is unseen is eternal" (2 Corinthians 4:18).

Paul is saying that you can't trust your physical vision. You can't trust what you see and the decisions you make based on that. You need to fix your eyes—by fixing your gaze. Your gaze is broken, but when you focus on the right things, it can be fixed.

The journey that you are about to take over the next forty days will open your eyes to what is going on beyond the seen . . . beyond the obvious. You will start to see what is really there and what is really going on. And you will be empowered to change for the better.

You may not be happy with your story right now. But, together we will uncover what has been hidden in plain sight. With faith as your lens, you will discover a whole new way of looking at the world. After all, when you can see the invisible, you can do the impossible.

    ✗ Think about the blind-spots you might have when it comes to understanding what is going on in the spiritual realm. Is it easy or hard for you to believe that these unseen things are as real as what is seen in the physical world? Why?

✗ With faith as your lens, you can see the invisible and do the impossible. What is something you would like to do right now that seems impossible?

✗ How do you want to improve your story over the course of this study and really begin to take back your life?

Day 2

||

IDENTITY CRISIS

 I pray that out of his glorious riches he may strengthen you with power through his Spirit in your inner being.

Ephesians 3:16

Before you can do the great things that God has called you to do, you have to first get things squared away on the inside. I am talking about *winning the war within*. As we have seen, this starts by recognizing a battle is taking place . . . that something is going on inside of you.

I like how the apostle Paul put it: "I don't really understand myself, for I want to do what is right, but I don't do it. Instead, I do what I hate" (Romans 7:15 NLT). I love that statement. Can't you picture Paul looking in the mirror, being like, *Who are you? I don't even know you.* He goes on to write, "I love God's law with all my heart. But there is another power within me that is at war with my mind" (verses 22–23 NLT).

We're all dealing with the civil war inside our souls. We are not completely sure what's the right thing to do. We have a great need for what Paul prayed for the church at Ephesus, that they would be strengthened in the inner being, according to the riches of his glory (Ephesians 3:16).

That's my prayer for you—that at the very outset of this journey, God would strengthen you in your inner being. That he will walk with you as we get wise to these battles and take back ground from the enemy.

If this feels like the start of an identity crisis for you . . . that's good! The best kind of crisis that you can have is an identity crisis, because this begins the process of learning who you truly are. That's why I want to push you into an identity crisis. It's the only place you can truly experience the relentless love of God.

- Paul expressed to the believers in Rome that he wanted to do right, but sometimes couldn't because there was another power at war within him. Where do you most experiencing this struggle? How does it make you feel about yourself?

- What lies have you been believing about your identity? How do they contrast with who God says you truly are?

- Where do you most need God to strengthen you today in your inner being?

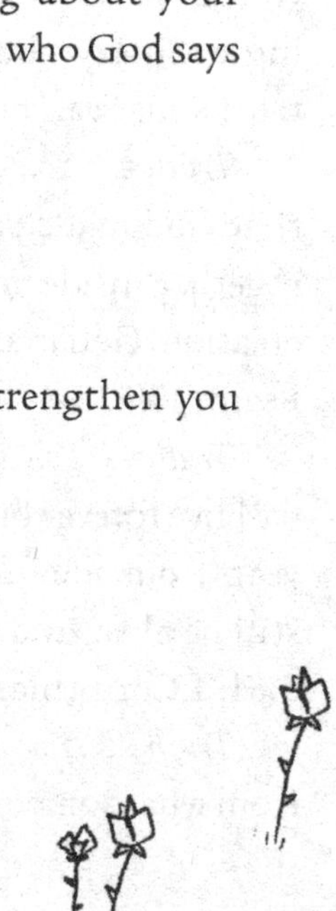

YOU MATTER MORE THAN YOU KNOW

 God created mankind in his own image,
in the image of God he created them;
male and female he created them.

Genesis 1:27

I don't know what you see when you look in the mirror, but if you are like me, there is a list of things you wish you could change. Regardless of what you see looking back at you when you brush your teeth, I can tell you that to God, there is nothing ordinary about you. The following are three critical truths that can help you see yourself as God sees you.

Truth #1: You are made in the image of God. The Bible said that God made you. He fearfully and wonderfully knit you together inside your mother. You're no accident. Out of all creation, God made you to be like him (see Genesis 1:27; 5:2; Psalm 139:13–14).

Truth #2: You are immortal. The question is not *whether* you will live forever but *where* you will live forever. Four hundred years from now—and four thousand years after that—you will still be alive, and you will still be you (see Luke 20:36; John 8:51; 1 Corinthians 15).

Truth #3. You are valuable. The value of something comes from what someone is willing to pay for it. The Bible says that while you were dead in your sins, God demonstrated his love for you by sending his Son to die for you (see Romans 5:8).

I hope you're starting to get a sense of how wildly unordinary you are. You were put on this earth to make waves, disrupt the status quo, and kick over some stinking applecarts.

✗ Which of these three truths is hardest for you to embrace? Why?

✗ In what ways would remembering you are made in God's image, are immortal, and are valuable change your approach the struggles of today?

✗ You were put on this earth to make waves and disrupt the status quo. Based on your unique story and interests, where can you begin doing this?

Day 4

||||

TORTURED GENIUS

 We are his workmanship, created in Christ Jesus
for good works, which God prepared beforehand,
that we should walk in them.

Ephesians 2:10 ESV

I have some good news for you. *You are a genius.* Yes, *you.* You were created by a Creator to create. You were put on this earth by a creative God to be creative and to dream things into existence.

God has tucked this genius within you. You're like an X-man. You're awesome. Now, like a great cosmic scavenger hunt, he wants you to figure out the nuanced way he has put this creative spark into your heart. As you do this, you will be able to execute one-of-a kind acts of genius that will fill your heart with passion and serve the people in your world.

Okay, now that I've given you the good news, I have some bad news. *You are a genius.* It's bad news because works of genius often come through great pain. You have to go through agony to birth something into the world that wasn't there before. It will cost you to create. There is conflict in every calling and angst inherent to the creative process.

But stay with it. Success isn't the immediate goal. Obedience is. And that begins with knowing who you are and doing what God calls you to do.

✖ How do you respond to the idea that you are a genius? Have you ever considered yourself that way? Why or why not?

✖ If you embraced the truth that God created you with the genes of his genius, how would that impact your pursuit of what you love to do?

✖ How have you experienced the cost for your creativity?

Day 5

IHHT

IF YOU SAY SO

 The LORD ... brought them to the man to see what he would name them; and whatever the man called each living creature, that was its name.

Genesis 2:19

The first job God gave humans back in the Garden of Eden was to speak a word over something that he made. Whatever Adam called the animal, as the Bible states, "that was its name." Adam's job was to speak ... and what he spoke *stuck*.

You have the same job. God brings a day to you, and your job is to give it a name and declare something over it. Whatever you call it will stick. This begins with what you say to the person each morning when you look into the mirror. Do you name the person you see *beautiful* or *ugly*? *Valuable* or *not worthy of love*? *Ready* for a tremendous day or already *behind*?

Whatever you say over what you see ... that is what it's called. The reality that is your words can unlock a life you love or a life you loathe. It is up to you whether the self-fulfilling prophecies you articulate become a delight or a dungeon.

So, as you start taking back your life, one of the first jobs you have is to speak life over yourself, just as Adam did. You can alter how you feel by changing what you say. As you do this, when you look in the mirror, you'll begin to see you as you were meant to be.

✖ Why do you think God gives our words so much power?

✖ What words or phrases do you tend to speak over yourself? How do you think that impacts your day?

✖ Have you gotten so good at listening to yourself that you've forgotten you can speak to yourself? What words do you most need to say to yourself to take back your life?

MASK OFF

For our boast is this, the testimony of our conscience,
that we behaved in the world with simplicity
and godly sincerity, not by earthly wisdom
but by the grace of God.

2 Corinthians 1:12 ESV

Think for a moment about the image you portray to others. Is that image that you're showing people really you? Or it is a little disguised? A little distorted? A little . . . masklike?

If so, you're not alone. God tells us in the Bible who we really are—valuable, important, powerful in him—but when the crises of life come our way, it can be so easy for us to forget. It's tempting in moments of pain or uncertainty to just slap on a mask as a defense. We want to hide the fears that we aren't pretty enough, rich enough, strong enough, or smart enough.

It's ironic that when we put on these masks in the hopes of finding love and acceptance, it prevents people from seeing the truth. After all, you can't love someone you don't know. What people are falling in love with isn't the real *you.* It's your mask, a superficial version of yourself, a costume you've carefully curated.

In the end, what you put on to obtain you must continue to wear to retain. If you got the job with the mask, you have to wear the mask every day at work. If you got the relationship with the mask, you have to wear the mask whenever you're with that person. But the kicker is that when you put on a mask, you are masking yourself from God's blessing.

The cure for insecurity is understanding your true identity. Don't miss this! You are unique. You are a beautiful work of art. You are God's masterpeice. You are what he thinks . . . not what you think. When you know who you really are, it doesn't matter what you are not.

You might have worn your mask for so long you no longer know what life looks like without it. But let me tell you . . . it looks like freedom.

✖ In what situations are you most likely to put on a mask? When you do, what are you usually trying to hide?

✖ When you fake it to make it, you have to keep faking it to make it. When has this happened to you? What was the outcome?

✖ What would it look like to always embrace your identity and stop wearing masks?

PERMISSION SLIP

 God gave us a spirit not of fear but of
power and love and self-control.

2 Timothy 1:7 ESV

It takes bravery to take off your mask and be vulnerable—
whether that is with yourself, others, or even with God. It's
not easy, and you will undoubtedly experience fear. You will
want to put the mask back on and hide once more.

But in every area of life, the only way to get to victory is
by going through vulnerability. I will give it to you straight.
When you choose against vulnerability, what you are really
choosing is *cowardice* and *fear.*

Now, I know this about you, without even knowing you:
fear is not a good look for you. It doesn't fit you. It wasn't
given to you. Paul said as much when he wrote about this to
Timothy. He knew his younger protégé was feeling afraid as
he pastored the church at Ephesus. This is why Paul reminded
him, "God didn't give you that spirit of fear."

Back in school, teachers would send home permission
slips if you wanted to go on a class field trip. Well, today I am
sending you with a permission slip to go on a different kind
of trip . . . a trip that leads to empowerment. This is your
permission slip to let everything go that isn't from God, and
he didn't give you a spirit of fear. So you can let it drop.

Remember, if God didn't give it to you, you don't have to keep it.

✗ What are some of the obstacles that make vulnerability difficult for you?

✗ When you don't choose vulnerability, you choose fear. What has the impact of that been in your life?

✗ You have permission to let go of anything that isn't from God. What is the first thing you will release?

For Next Week: Use the space below and on the following page to write any insights or questions that you want to discuss at the next group meeting. In preparation for next week, review week 2 in *Take Back Your Life*.

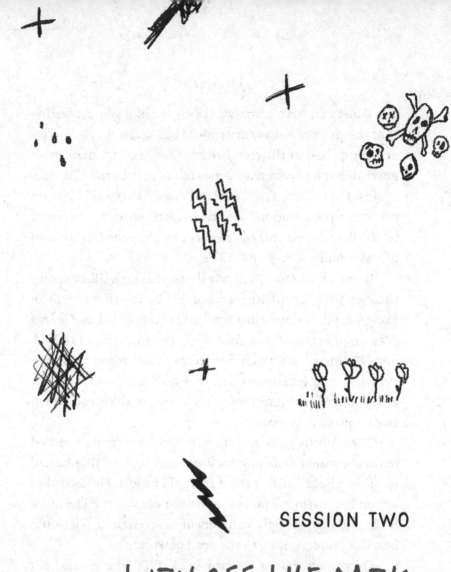

tURN OFF tHE DARK

Things are not always what they seem: the first appearance deceives many; the intelligence of a few perceives what has been carefully hidden.

Gaius Julius Phaedrus

WELCOME

The American Revolution was born out of a general feeling that things were not as they should be. At the time, America was comprised of thirteen British colonies, and the British government had enacted a series of tax acts to fund its wars against the French. The colonists believed this was "taxation without representation," and this—along with other actions by the British—ultimately led them to issue the Declaration of Independence on July 4, 1776.

It was a bold move, and one that didn't go well at first for the colonists. The British responded by landing troops in Long Island, forcing the Continental Army, led by George Washington, out of New York. More reinforcements arrived, and Washington was chased across New Jersey and into Pennsylvania. Numerous defeats led to poor morale in the army, and Washington was faced with widespread desertions among his troops.

The months passed, and the British army finally settled in for the winter. Washington knew at this point that he had to make a bold move or the war would be lost. He needed to act on his instincts, mobilize his army, cross the Delaware River, and take the fight to his enemy . . . even though it would be a risky undertaking in the dead of winter.

On the evening of December 25, 1776, the general put whatever hesitations he had behind him and ordered his troops into the boats. The night crossing was made worse by the arrival of a strong storm that brought freezing rain, snow, and strong winds, but the Continental Army persevered and landed on the other side. The rest, as they say, is history. Washington led his troops against the British and caught them off guard. As the victories mounted over the next few days, so did his troops' morale. This singular event served to turn the tide of the war.

The Bible reveals that things are likewise not as they should be in this world. There is disease, death, darkness, and an enemy that seeks to defeat us. We can quickly become demoralized when we consider all we are facing. Yet it is during these times that God calls us to confront the darkness and cross to the other side. As we will discuss in this session, he wants us to lean into what we are feeling, operate in his power, and work to take back our lives.

SHARE

If you or any of your group members are just getting to know one another, take a few minutes to introduce yourselves and share any insights you have from last week's personal study. Then, to kick things off, discuss one of the following questions:

♢ When are some times that you felt demoralized by what you were facing?

— *or* —

♢ How have you sensed that things are "not as they should be" in this world?

READ

Invite someone to read aloud the following passage. Listen for fresh insights as you hear the verses being read, and then discuss the questions that follow.

The Spirit God gave us does not make us timid, but gives us power, love and self-discipline. So do not be ashamed of the testimony about our Lord or of me his prisoner. Rather, join with me in suffering for the gospel, by the power of God. He has saved us and called us to a holy life—not because of anything we have done but because of his own purpose and grace. This grace was given us in Christ Jesus before the beginning of time, but it has now been revealed through the appearing of our Savior, Christ Jesus, who has destroyed death and has brought life and immortality to light through the gospel. And of this gospel I was appointed a herald and an apostle and a teacher. That is why I am suffering as I am. Yet this is no cause for shame, because I know whom I have believed, and am convinced that he is able to guard what I have entrusted to him until that day.

What you heard from me, keep as the pattern of sound teaching, with faith and love in Christ Jesus. Guard the good deposit that was entrusted to you—guard it with the help of the Holy Spirit who lives in us (2 Timothy 1:7-14).

What key insight stands out to you from this passage?

What does Paul say about what Jesus has accomplished in this world?

WATCH

Play the video segment for session two. As you watch, fill in the blanks in the following outline and also record any thoughts or concepts that stand out to you.

NOTES

There are unseen forces that pull at a compass needle. These forces were there long before it was invented. The compass didn't create those forces . . . it just revealed them.

We need God to give us the ability to sense what he has put into all of us—like a compass inside our souls that can help us to navigate through this life and through this world.

The Bible reveals the world is "groaning" because everything is not as it should be. We know there is great beauty in this world . . . but we also recognize something is missing.

God is trying to tell us through the groaning of this world—and the groaning inside of our hearts—that we were meant for *more*. We were meant for heaven.

The Holy Spirit, through his groaning in our hearts, helps us to know what to pray for and how to interact in a relationship with God. He "pushes the doorbell" so we will open our hearts.

We should respond to this groaning in our hearts not by *fighting* it but by *leaning into* it. How should we respond to this groaning we sense in our hearts?

Three things will happen as we lean into the groaning and let God work in our hearts:

First, *we discover a better way to evaluate life.*

Second, *we are lifted up and get a higher perspective on our situation.*

Third, *we gain the traction to not slip and fall in this life.*

When we are responding to the Holy Spirit's groan in our hearts, we always have a compass to guide us to the things that he has called us to do.

DISCUSS

Take a few minutes with your group members to discuss what you just watched and explore these concepts together.

1. What helps you navigate through life—especially through the dark times?

2. When was the first time you interacted with death? How did your relationship with God affect the way you handled that experience?

3. Read Romans 8:22–27. What do you think is the purpose of the Holy Spirit's groaning? How does the Holy Spirit help you in your weakness?

4. How can you better respond to the groaning of the Holy Spirit in your heart?

5. How has the "groaning" in your heart helped you to better evaluate your life?

6. How has the "groaning" in your heart helped you to get better perspective on your situation and provided you the traction you needed to get through it?

RESPOND

Briefly review the outline for the video teaching and any notes you took. In the space below, write down the most significant point you took away from this session.

PRAY

Wrap up your time together by taking a few minutes to talk with God. Here are a few ideas of what you could pray about based on what you discussed in this session:

- Ask God to continually help you sense his presence in your life.
- Pray that you can lean into the Holy Spirit as you get to know God better.
- Thank God for his love for you and for his desire to lead you.
- Declare your resolve to look at life through the higher perspective that you have received in Christ.

BETWEEN-SESSIONS PERSONAL STUDY

Before you begin this personal study, you may want to review week 2 in *Take Back Your Life*. Be sure to also read the reflection questions after each activity and make a few notes in your guide about the experience. Once again, there will be a few minutes for you to share any insights you learned at the start of the next session.

Day 8

𝍦 𝍩

JESUS TURNS OFF
THE DARK

 Jesus . . . has destroyed death and has brought life and immortality to light through the gospel.

2 Timothy 1:10

It was December 20, 2012, and I was working on my Christmas message. I had gotten the idea for it a few weeks before, when my wife, Jennie, and I were in New York to see the Spider-Man musical with friends. As I walked out of the theater, lightning struck when I saw the big, bold letters on the marquee: *"Spider-Man: Turn Off the Dark."*

The words had tumbled around in my mind, over and over. It's an unusual phrase. You would usually say, "Turn *on* the light." You generally don't think about darkness being deactivated. But there we were, in Times Square, with all the chaos and flashing lights everywhere, and it hit me. "Eureka!" I announced to no one in particular. "There's my Christmas message! Turn off the dark."

The truth is that Jesus came into this world to turn off the darkness of death by turning on the light. As the author of Hebrews states, he came to release those "who all their lives were held in slavery by their fear of death" (2:15). Christmas exists so there can be an Easter . . . so we can live with hope and die without fear.

This is why we can rise above fear, pain, bondage, even death. Jesus is turning off the dark all around us. And what we see in the light changes everything.

✗ How do you respond to the idea that Christmas exists so there can be an Easter?

✗ What is a recent example of how Jesus turned off the dark in your life?

✗ What are some ways that Jesus has freed you from fear in your life?

ꟼꟼꟼ ||||

NOT FINISHED YET

 He too shared in their humanity so that by his death he might
break the power of him who holds the power of death.

Hebrews 2:14

If you're curious how Jesus feels about grief and death, just take a look at how viscerally he reacted to the death of his friend Lazarus.

Jesus didn't hide his emotion or try to disguise his sadness. He didn't put sunglasses on or clumsily say, "It's okay! Lazarus has gone to a better place, everybody. He's probably playing football in my Father's house." No, rather, "Jesus wept" (John 11:35).

The Bible says twice that Jesus groaned in his spirit (see John 11:33, 38 NKJV). This was no ordinary sigh. The Greek word used here means to "bellow with rage." It is normally used to describe the angry snorting of an agitated horse. So much for gentle Jesus. He was absolutely outraged—mad at death, the grave, sin, and the devil.

Jesus was angry enough at death to do something about it. He went on to defeat death in the most unlikely way ever— by dying himself. Jesus used death, Satan's most powerful weapon, against him. The dark has been switched off forever. As the apostle Paul put it, "[Jesus], having disarmed the powers and authorities . . . made a public spectacle of them, triumphing over them by the cross" (Colossians 2:15).

In this life, it may seem as if death has won. But remember that God's not finished yet. The final destruction of death is still in the future. It hasn't happened yet . . . but it will.

✗ What stands out most to you about how Jesus reacted to the death of Lazarus?

✗ What hope do you have in knowing that Jesus has conquered death?

✗ Why should Jesus' defeat of death give you an unwavering hope in any circumstance?

Day 10

HHH THL

SPIRITUAL LENSES

Jesus spoke to them, saying,
"I am the light of the world. Whoever follows me will not
walk in darkness, but will have the light of life."
John 8:12 ESV

None of us pursues loss and suffering. Yet God has a unique way of using the tragic times in our lives for his unique purposes. Grief has the ability to enhance our spiritual senses.

It is in the incredibly difficult moments of life that the unseen spiritual world becomes more vivid and we sense the nearness of God's kingdom in ways that we've never experienced before. God's whisper is often amplified in the deafening roar of death and loss.

I suppose this is what Jesus meant when he said, "Blessed are those who mourn" (Matthew 5:4). He gives us gifts in the midst of grief that we would not have had the bandwidth to receive if everything in our lives was going as planned.

It's like a misaligned lens deep in our souls is suddenly jolted into place. Without this lens, we can't see what's there. But when we believe and see what God says is there, we start looking at life through the lens of faith. This corrected lens will change everything.

Jesus gives us new lenses. He is the light of the world that bounces off them and makes everything around us illuminated. Walking forward with his light in our eyes, we will start to see eternity. We will see the world differently. The dark won't stand a chance.

x What recent event in your life has enhanced your spiritual senses?

x How does looking through the lens of faith change how you see your current reality?

x What are some ways that you might partner with Jesus—the light of the world—to help turn off the dark for others?

Day 11
̵H̵T̵ ̵H̵L̵ I

BREAD AND CIRCUSES

 So that we would not be outwitted by Satan;
for we are not ignorant of his designs.

2 Corinthians 2:11 ESV

You are special and destined for impact. You are living in the present but made for eternity. In addition, you have a unique calling on your life. Unfortunately, God is not the only one who knows this about you. Your enemy, the devil, knows it as well, and he is desperate to keep you from realizing it and reaching your potential.

Satan's strategy is similar to what the Romans did in Jesus' time to control the citizens of their empire. You might call this strategy "bread and circuses." Basically, the Roman emperors found that as long as they kept their people fed and entertained, they didn't complain too much about the fact they were stealing their freedoms. Free food and endless entertainment—bread and circuses—kept people amused while their liberty was taken.

The devil is all about "bread and circuses." He wants you to give up what Christ died for you to have. He knows that if he can distract you, he can destroy you. It's a rather ingenious strategy, actually, because it's so difficult to detect when it's happening. It often doesn't involve *bad things* but *good things* that take the place of the most *important things*.

You do not have to fall for Satan's tricks. Open your eyes! Use your lenses! Life is more than what so-and-so tweeted, which celebrities just broke up, and what the latest and greatest food truck is serving up. You were meant to live on a higher level.

x What are some ways you have seen the enemy use the strategy of "bread and circuses" against you or people you know?

x Sometimes, good things can distract you from important things. What is an example of where you pursued (or settled for) the good only to miss the better God had for you?

x Paul writes that we are not ignorant of Satan's designs (see 2 Corinthians 2:11). How can this awareness keep you from falling prey to his strategies?

Day 12

||||| ||||| ||

THE HARM OF BEING
A HYBRID

 Our citizenship is in heaven, and from it we await
a Savior, the Lord Jesus Christ.

Philippians 3:20 ESV

In the early 1990s, the Chhatbir Zoo in India conducted a breeding experiment between Asiatic and African lions. The zoo administrators, looking to devise a special attraction, decided to mix the two together . . . but it backfired. When the hybrid cubs were born, their back legs were too weak to support them. Some were so feeble they couldn't even eat meat off the bone and had to be served boneless meat.

This sad story is what is at stake if we don't fight to keep our hearts set on heaven. If the enemy can get us to mix enough compromise into our lives, he will be able to slip a muzzle over our snouts. God intends for us to be a people who can "run and not grow weary . . . walk and not be faint" (Isaiah 40:31). Compromise with the enemy weakens our faith and makes us so feeble we aren't be able to stand against him.

In Paul's letter to the Philippians, he said that followers of Christ are not to focus only on earthly things because their citizenship is in heaven (see 3:19-20). We can't focus on the distractions of this world and on the riches of heaven at the same time. We are not meant to be a hybrid of those two kinds of "lions."

So, refuse to live a life that is weak, muzzled, and ineffective. Instead, fix your eyes on the true Lion. As you do, you will see through the lies of the enemy and avoid his schemes.

- How can a "hybrid" life weaken you spiritually and impact your witness for Christ?

- What are ways that you have been tempted to compromise with the enemy?

- In what ways could you *take back your life* if you saw your time here on earth as simply being a long layover to another, far better, and permanent destination?

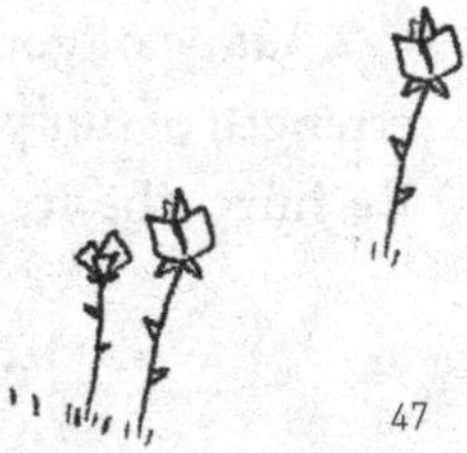

PAIN IS A MICROPHONE

No one should be shaken by these afflictions;
for you yourselves know that we are appointed to this.

1 Thessalonians 3:3 NKJV

It was the loss of William Wallace's wife that led him from being a simple farmer in Scotland to a revolutionary against the unjust English powers of his day. Without this anguish in his life, he would have just been another guy in a kilt. Truly, pain is a microphone.

The Bible also says that pain is *guaranteed*. "He causes his sun to rise on the evil and the good, and sends rain on the righteous and the unrighteous" (Matthew 5:45). Part of living on this fallen planet, cursed by sin, is that trials are inherent. It's just the way it is. Pain comes with the territory.

Furthermore, as children of God, the difficulties ramp up to a whole other level. Why? Well, as Uncle Ben of *Spider-Man* fame once said to his younger nephew, "With great power comes great responsibility." The enemy of our soul is not going to let us capture his flag without some serious flak. This is why Paul told his younger coworker Timothy, "Everyone who wants to live a godly life in Christ Jesus will be persecuted" (2 Timothy 3:12).

But be of good cheer. There is a connection between the strength of our pain and the volume of our voices. The more we hurt, the louder we become. Our pain can serve as a microphone that ministers to others and draws them to Christ. So let nothing be wasted.

My prayer for all the grief you have experienced is that God would help you to see that there is *power in the pain*. Suffering is not an obstacle to being used by God. Rather, it can be an opportunity to be used by him like never before.

✗ How does it make you feel that pain is *guaranteed* in the life of a believer?

✗ How have you seen God use a bad situation for his good?

✗ Who could benefit today from your story of pain?

Day 14

HHT HHL IIII

THE WAR ON DARKNESS

 Set your minds on things above, not on earthly things.

Colossians 3:2

Jesus has turned off the dark. He has vanquished death. He has given us citizenship in heaven. He has provided us with new lenses to see the invisible and a microphone in our pain.

Here is where it gets dangerous. Now that Jesus has turned off the dark eternally, we get to join him in turning it off here on earth. Because we see with spiritual eyes, we get to declare war on the darkness in all its forms—wherever it occurs, either outside us or inside us.

I have no doubt the devil sends demons to mess with me. The world might very well be another source of problems that come at me. But this I know for sure: *I cause more than enough problems to keep myself occupied.* But no matter where problems are coming from, I have made a decision. I have chosen to *declare war.* On darkness. On my demons. On my self-sabotaging tendencies and my selfishness. I declare war on darkness.

When you choose to declare war, you are refusing to go gently in the night or to be taken without a fight. You are declaring war on the version of yourself that you don't want to be. You're choosing a different direction. You're choosing to reclaim your thoughts and actions.

During the rest of our journey, you will discover that you have a lot of firepower at your disposal. God has not only provided you with lenses to help you see what is going on around you, but he has also given you the backing to do something about it. So, declare war on the darkness. Get out of your own way . . . and step into the life you were born to live.

✗ What are you most uncertain about in declaring war on darkness?

✗ What are you most excited about in making this declaration?

✗ Write your declaration of war in the space below. It doesn't need to be long or complicated. You want it short so you can remember it. Focus on areas that the enemy, the world, and your flesh cause you to stumble. Make it personal.

For Next Week: Use the space below and on the following page to write any insights or questions that you want to discuss at the next group meeting. In preparation for next week, review week 3 in *Take Back Your Life*.

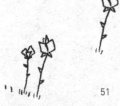

SESSION THREE

CROSS THE BARBED WIRE

War must be, while we defend our lives against
a destroyer who would devour all.

J.R.R. Tolkien

WELCOME

When it comes to making cross-the-line-and-never-look-back decisions, few in the modern era stand up to the one that John F. Kennedy made back in 1962. The youngest president in the nation's history had entered office scarcely a year before. At the time, America was embroiled in what has been called the "Cold War" with the Soviet Union, with each side threatening nuclear war against the other in an attempt to keep the balance of power in the world.

The crisis began when a U-2 spy plane made a high-altitude pass over Cuba on October 14 and photographed a Soviet medium-range ballistic missile being assembled for installation. Given the proximity of Cuba to the coast of Florida—a little more than 100 miles away—the missiles could reach targets in the eastern United States. Kennedy was apprised of the situation two days later and quickly assembled a team to determine a course of action.

It was not an easy decision. If the country did nothing, the United States would be vulnerable to attack and the Soviets would be emboldened to make even greater moves. But if the country acted, it could lead to an immediate full-scale nuclear war. Kennedy ultimately decided that in spite of the risk, a line in the sand had to be drawn—or, more accurately, a line in the ocean. On October 22, Kennedy ordered the U.S. Navy to establish a blockade, or "quarantine," of the island to prevent the Soviets from delivering additional missiles.

The tense standoff lasted into the next week. Soviet ships approached the blockade on October 24. Then an American reconnaissance plane was shot down over Cuba on October 27. The president ordered an invasion force to be assembled in Florida. Finally, on October 28, the Soviets agreed to remove the missiles in Cuba in exchange for a promise that the United States would not invade the island nation. The crisis was over.

In our lives, we will also be confronted with such cross-the-barbed-wire type decisions. At such times, we have to decide whether we are going to play it safe or refuse to submit to the enemy's tactics. While our response will (hopefully) not carry the weight of the one made by the United States during the Cuban Missile Crisis, we can be certain that it *will* involve risk. Furthermore, the battlefield for this fight will often take place in our own minds.

SHARE

Begin your group time by inviting those in the group to share their insights from last week's personal study. Then, to kick things off, discuss one of the following questions:

- When is a time that you had to make a decision that involved great risk?

— *or* —

- How do you determine the best course of action when you have to make a tough decision that you know will impact others?

READ

Invite someone to read aloud the following passage. Listen for fresh insights as you hear the verses being read, and then discuss the questions that follow.

*By the humility and gentleness of Christ, I appeal to you—
I, Paul, who am "timid" when face to face with you, but
"bold" toward you when away! I beg you that when I come
I may not have to be as bold as I expect to be toward some
people who think that we live by the standards of this world.
For though we live in the world, we do not wage war as the
world does. The weapons we fight with are not the weapons
of the world. On the contrary, they have divine power to demolish strongholds. We demolish arguments and every pre-
tension that sets itself up against the knowledge of God, and
we take captive every thought to make it obedient to Christ.
And we will be ready to punish every act of disobedience,
once your obedience is complete* (2 Corinthians 10:1–6).

What key insight stands out to you from this passage?

How does Paul reveal that he is ready to "do battle" with
those who oppose him? How does he describe the nature of
the battle that he knows he is waging?

WATCH

Play the video segment for session three. As you watch, fill in the blanks in the following outline and also record any thoughts or concepts that stand out to you.

NOTES

In this war, there comes a time when we must refuse to stay pinned down and take the fight to our enemy. As we do, we will experience the "power of the wolf" rising up in our hearts.

This warrior spirit compels us to leave the safety of our comfort zone and move into the unknown, uncertain, and uncharted terrain that is the adventure of following Jesus.

Crossing over the "barbed wire" will require us to tear down strongholds the enemy has constructed in our lives and begin to *think like a wolf*.

We dwell on thoughts that are positive.

We dwell on thoughts that are beautiful.

Tearing down strongholds will also require us to begin to *speak like a wolf.*

We speak words that encourage others rather than tear them down.

We speak words that will encourage and coach ourselves.

Tearing down strongholds will also require us to begin to *act like a wolf.*

We work with others in our "pack" as part of a team.

We take control of our posture and pregame.

Tearing down strongholds will also require us to begin to *fight like a wolf.* We allow the Holy Spirit to fill us with power and actively engage in the fight.

No one can fight this battle for us. If we want to cross the "barbed wire," we must take the first step as we rely on the Spirit of God within us. As we do, the wolf will rise.

DISCUSS

Take a few minutes with your group members to discuss what you just watched and explore these concepts together.

1. What are some reasons why people might choose to "play it safe" when it comes to living out their faith? When have you been tempted to just play it safe in life?

2. Read Matthew 14:22–32. What risks did Peter take in this story? How do you think this impacted his faith in Jesus as the Son of God?

3. Read 2 Corinthians 10:3–5. How would you define a *stronghold* based on this passage? Why is it critical for these strongholds to be demolished in your life?

4. What kind of thoughts do you need to start thinking to tear down strongholds?

5. What kind of words do you need to start saying to yourself and to others?

6. What kind of actions to do you need to start taking? How have you seen the power of the Holy Spirit enable you to take the fight to the enemy?

RESPOND

Briefly review the outline for the video teaching and any notes you took. In the space below, write down the most significant point you took away from this session.

PRAY

Wrap up your time together by taking a few minutes to talk with God. Here are a few ideas of what you could pray about based on what you discussed in this session:

- Ask God to break down any strongholds that keep you from moving forward in obedience to him.
- Pray for the courage to be bold as you take risks in the adventure of following Jesus.
- Thank God for the power of his Spirit to help you move forward in confidence.
- Declare your commitment to train your thoughts and use your words and actions to fight for what God wants for you.

BETWEEN-SESSIONS PERSONAL STUDY

Before you begin this personal study, you may want to review week 3 in *Take Back Your Life*. Be sure to also read the reflection questions after each activity and make a few notes in your guide about the experience. Once again, there will be a few minutes for you to share any insights you learned at the start of the next session.

꜀꜀꜀꜀꜀ ꜀꜀꜀꜀꜀ ꜀꜀꜀꜀꜀

OVER THE LINE

Be strong and courageous, and do the work.
Do not be afraid or discouraged, for the LORD God, my God,
is with you. He will not fail you or forsake you.

1 Chronicles 28:20

When you decide you're done being pushed around by darkness in your life, and you're ready to become a victor, you will find that a wolf rises in your heart. This is how Theodore Roosevelt—the larger-than-life president chiseled in stone on Mount Rushmore—described the "power of joy in battle" that floods a person who chooses to meet great challenges.

Roosevelt experienced this "rising of the wolf" in his heart when he led the Rough Riders on horseback into the battle for San Juan Hill during the Spanish-American War. Machine gun bullets sprayed out from the top of the mountain, cutting down man after man, yet Teddy fought on, relentlessly urging his men forward. At one point, he saw a barbed-wire fence that lay across the battlefield. This was the moment that changed everything for him.

As death surrounded him, amid danger and fear, he drew the line inside himself. He made the decision to not turn back. A switch flipped inside, and he became unstoppable in his resolve. For the rest of his life, he referred to that day—July 1, 1898—as the greatest day of his life. The day the wolf rose in his heart.

There is great power that comes when you likewise choose to cross the barbed wire and take the fight to the enemy. It's at this point that you *stop letting life happen to you and start happening to your life*. You declare war . . . and on that day, the wolf rises within you.

✖ How do you describe the "power of joy in battle" when you are faced with a difficult challenge that you must overcome?

✖ What does it look like to *stop letting life happen to you and start happening to your life*?

✖ What is holding you back from doing this—and what are you going to do about it?

Day 16

A HOSTAGE SITUATION

Because of the LORD's great love we are not consumed,
for his compassions never fail. They are new every morning;
great is your faithfulness.

Lamentations 3:22–23

Where did we get the idea that one bad decision must be followed by another? Maybe it comes from failing to understand the true meaning of this often-quoted verse in Lamentations.

Jeremiah *isn't* saying a new morning is the only time we have the opportunity to receive mercy. There isn't anything mystical attached to the clock striking midnight. Rather, we have the opportunity to go to God morning, noon, and night—once a day, nine times a day, every hour if we need to—and claim the help we need for the present struggle we are facing.

As the author of Hebrews says, "So let us boldly approach God's throne of grace. Then we will receive mercy. We will find grace to help us when we need it" (4:16 NIRV). We don't have to wait for the start of day. We needn't write off a day that has been tainted. We can start over on the spot. We can seek the grace of God *when we need it!*

So shake your internal Etch A Sketch. Embrace the brand-new mercies just waiting for you. Only pride and silliness allow a bad decision to turn into a bad day and make you defer until tomorrow what you need to do right now. Don't let your spirit be held hostage by previous bad decisions or failures. Brand-new mercies are ready to rescue you . . . right now.

✗ How do you typically respond when you make a bad decision? Do you feel like the entire day is blown? Why or why not?

✗ Why is it often so hard to boldly approach God's throne of grace when we make mistakes—even though that is when we most need his grace?

✗ What new mercies would you like from God right now? List them below. Then pause and ask God for those mercies, knowing he will give them to you.

Day 17

‖‖‖ ‖‖‖ ‖‖‖ ‖‖

FLIP YOUR THOUGHTS

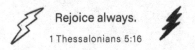

Rejoice always.

1 Thessalonians 5:16

I know a lot of people who sneer at the idea of positive thinking, as though it were somehow a betrayal of the gospel. But positive thinking isn't offensive to God. It's actually obedience to him. The shortest verse in the Bible (in the original Greek) makes that clear: "rejoice always."

Paul tells you specifically that ever-present joy is a part of God's plan for your life: "Rejoice always, pray continually, give thanks in all circumstances; for this is God's will for you in Christ Jesus" (1 Thessalonians 5:16–18). With these commands—*rejoice, pray, give thanks*—he is not only telling you the will of God but also giving you tools to flip your thoughts.

When you feel like complaining, or see yourself acting selfishly, or find yourself slipping into a bad mood, shoot a prayer to God that is full of joy and gratitude. Setting your mind on things above you is declaring war on low-level thinking. This doesn't mean you have to be thankful *for* everything—like death or divorce or unemployment. Those things aren't good. You can, however, be thankful *in everything*—or in any other thing hell can throw at you—because God has a plan to produce good from what you are facing.

You have the ability to reverse negative to positive. You can flip your mind and make it stick. They don't call it a *mindset* for no reason. You have to actually set your mind. Just give it a try.

✗ Does it seem naïve to embrace positive thinking, given the problems in this world? If so, why do you think Paul commands you to rejoice at all times?

✗ What would it look like for you to give thanks *in* everything you are going through?

✗ In your current challenges, how can you flip your thoughts using the tools that Paul provides—rejoicing, praying, and giving thanks?

Day 18

IIII IIII IIII III

MIND YOUR WORDS

The tongue has the power of life and death,
and those who love it will eat its fruit.

Proverbs 18:21

The tongue has the power of both *life* and *death*. James echoed the words of this proverb in his letter when he wrote, "Out of the same mouth come praise and cursing" (3:10). The tongue is like a tiny nuclear reactor that is capable of being both an energy plant that lights up a town (*praising*) and a bomb that can destroy a city (*cursing*).

All things that can do much good can also do great evil. Bricks can be used to build hospitals or be thrown through windows. Water can quench a thirst or flood a city. Fire can warm a room or burn down a house. Words are likewise neutral in and of themselves. It's how you use them that determines whether they are good or bad.

A sentence can devastate you: "We're going to have to let you go. It's cancer. There's nothing more we can do." Words can cost you your job. Just ask any number of talk show hosts. Words can cost you your life. Mouth off to the wrong person and you'll get yourself killed.

But words can just as easily cause you to celebrate: "You're being promoted! You have the golden ticket! Your long-lost aunt left you an enormous inheritance!" Whatever can be used for evil can be reclaimed and used for good. The tongue can be "set on fire by hell" (James 3:6), but it can also be set on fire by heaven.

On average, 16,000 words will come out of your mouth per day. Enlist all of them to help—not hinder—the cause for which you're fighting. Turn your mind to your words, and knowing their power, enlist them to your cause.

✗ How have your cutting or careless words gotten you in trouble in the past?

✗ The Bible says the tongue holds the power of life and death. How does that knowledge change the way in which you will use your words going forward?

✗ Of the 16,000 words that you will speak today, do you think it is possible for the majority of them to be words of life, peace, hope, mercy, and goodness? Why or why not?

Day 19

|||| |||| |||| ||||

CHANGE THE OUTCOME

 Truly I tell you, if you have faith as small as a mustard seed, you can say to this mountain, "Move from here to there," and it will move. Nothing will be impossible for you.

Matthew 17:20

In the Gospel of Matthew, we read that when Jesus healed the servant of a Roman centurion, he said to the man, "As you have believed, so *let it be* done for you" (8:13 NKJV). Faith is the password that unlocks God's power. This doesn't mean Jesus came to give us a blank check for any dream we have. But when hard days come, we have the promise that the way we speak in the midst of our crisis can cause something to happen that feels impossible.

The centurion had enough faith to ask for a long-distance miracle, and as a result, Jesus granted his request and moved the mountain. Likewise, in your life, a mountain of discouragement, ingrained negativity, or hopelessness *can* move. The impossible *will* happen because of how you speak about it. You determine to speak words of blessing. Of positivity. Of faith in God. Of encouragement to everyone you encounter.

How you speak can change the future and alter the course of history. When your words are full of faith, impossible things can be accomplished. Of course, this doesn't mean there won't be times when you speak words of faith and see nothing happen. In those moments, the most important thing is to remember that some of God's most important miracles can't be seen with the naked eye. Sometimes, the mountain that needs moving is inside of you.

> ✖ What feels like an unmovable mountain in your life right now?

> ✖ How do you respond to the idea that how you speak can change your future?

> ✖ Have you had a time when the mountain that needed moving was inside you? Do you view that miracle as important as the external mountains you want God to move?

Day 20

HH HH HH HH

TAKE BACK THE CONTROLS

 Tell the righteous that it shall be well with them, for they shall eat the fruit of their deeds.

Isaiah 3:10 ESV

Little by little we make our choices, and then our choices make us. As the philosopher Will Durant observed, "We are what we repeatedly do." Your habits either put the wind in your face or at your back. The right ones need to stay . . . and the wrong ones need to go.

One particularly bad habit that threatens our ability to achieve greatness is our addiction to our screens. Truly, the robots are taking over. Alexa. Siri. Automatic lane assist. It's a brave new world overflowing with automation. Americans today spend up to five hours a day on their phones. This means that almost a third of the time they're awake, they're hunched over glowing screens. That's 150 hours a month—or about fourteen years of our lives—checking emails, sending texts, playing games, and shopping online.

The habits you allow in your life today will determine who you become tomorrow. Future you will be an exaggerated version of current you. *Time won't change anything—it will merely deepen and reveal who you already are.* If you are kind today, you will be kinder tomorrow. If you are cruel today, that, too, will deepen. The choice is yours.

So choose well . . . and then use those new habits to break the old ones. Of course, this will feel uncomfortable for a while. It is always awkward to try something new. Your desire for comfort will beg you to go back to how it used to be. But you mustn't relent. Declare war on your bad habits, and then set good habits that will solidify over time into lifelong strengths.

✖ You make your choices, but your choices will make you. What choices are you currently making that are leading to a better you?

✖ Equally important, what choices are you currently making that are weakening you?

✖ Does the statement that future you will be an exaggerated version of current you bring you joy or fear? Why or why not?

Day 21

HHT HHT HHT HHT I

COMPOUND INTEREST

 With your help I can advance against a troop;
with my God I can scale a wall.

Psalm 18:29

There is no such thing as a small decision. Every time you make a decision, it's like a domino falling over. And everyone knows that one domino takes down the next.

In fact, physicist Hans van Leeuwen discovered that every time a domino falls, it generates a force sufficient to knock down a domino twice as big as itself. That means that in decisions—as in dominoes—one choice affects another. The effects of those choices accumulate and magnify over time. This is called exponential growth.

Understanding the mind-boggling phenomenon of exponential growth has the capacity to change every aspect of your life. In just a single decade, you can rack up a mountain of credit card debt, pack on thirty extra pounds, or smoke 36,500 cigarettes. On the flip side, you can use the time to become fluent in a new language, get a degree, and set yourself up to be financially stable and generous. Ten years is long enough to do a lot for good or for evil.

An old proverb says the best time to plant a tree is twenty years ago, but the second-best time is right now. So repeat after me: *the right time to do the right thing is right now.* Every second you stall is time that exponential growth could be working its slow magic. If you choose to delay until tomorrow what you should be doing today, you forfeit the opportunity to power through the necessary humble beginnings for another precious twenty-four hours.

There is not a moment to lose. The journey of a million miles has to start somewhere, and that somewhere is where you plant your shoe on the ground for the first time and believe that God will have your back. So, today, take that first step.

✗ Do you agree that there are no small decisions in life? Why or why not?

✗ How have you seen the principle of exponential growth play out in your life?

✗ What small step will you take today to start building exponential growth for the future?

For Next Week: Use the space below and on the following page to write any insights or questions that you want to discuss at the next group meeting. In preparation for next week, review week 4 in *Take Back Your Life*.

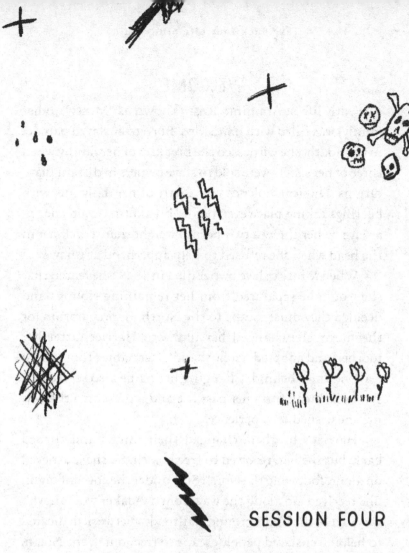

SESSION FOUR

RUN tOWARD tHE ROAR

Courage is not the absence of fear, but the triumph over it. The brave man is not he who does not feel afraid, but he who conquers that fear.

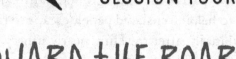

Nelson Mandela

WELCOME

The early life of Araminta Ross (known as "Minty" to her family) was filled with hardships. Born to enslaved parents in the South, she witnessed the breakup of her family when three of her sisters were sold to slave owners in distant plantations. Physical violence was a part of her daily life, with beatings taking place even before breakfast. As a teenager, a slave owner threw a two-pound weight that struck her in the head when she refused to help apprehend a runaway.

When Minty's slave owner died in 1849, she feared that she would be separated from her remaining siblings and decided they must escape to the North. In preparation for the move, she changed her name to Harriet (after her mother) and adopted her husband's last name (Tubman) to leave no trace behind. Changing her name also served as a symbolic break from her past life and represented the new life she wished to experience.

Harriet's brothers changed their minds and turned back, but she had resolved to free herself. So she journeyed on alone, following the North Star under the cover of night. She received aid along the way from a Quaker woman who was part of the Underground Railroad, a network dedicated to helping enslaved people escape to freedom in the North. Finally, after traveling nearly ninety miles, she arrived in "the land of freedom."

It would have been easy for Harriet Tubman at this point to have just remained there. But she felt God calling her to bring other enslaved people to freedom. So, at the risk of her own life, she returned to the South as a member of the Underground Railroad and began bringing out groups of slaves. During her nineteen trips, she led more than 300 people to freedom. Later, when the Civil War began, she became the first woman to lead an armed expedition, liberating more than 700 enslaved people in a raid at Combahee Ferry.

Harriet Tubman serves as an example of what it means to *take back your life* in the face of fear. She refused to "play it safe" and returned to the South to help other enslaved people. In the same way, as we will see in this session, God will often call us to face our fears when it comes to following his will. He calls us to act courageously . . . in spite of our fears.

SHARE

Begin your group time by inviting those in the group to share their insights from last week's personal study. Then, to kick things off, discuss one of the following questions:

* When is a time that you had to face your fears? What happened as a result?

— or —

* What are some ways recently that God has asked you to step out of your comfort zone? How have you responded to his call?

READ

Invite someone to read aloud the following passage. Listen for fresh insights as you hear the verses being read, and then discuss the questions that follow.

The LORD is my light and my salvation—
     whom shall I fear?
The LORD is the stronghold of my life—
     of whom shall I be afraid? . . .
Though an army besiege me,
     my heart will not fear;
though war break out against me,
     even then I will be confident.

One thing I ask from the LORD,
     this only do I seek:
that I may dwell in the house of the LORD
     all the days of my life,
to gaze on the beauty of the LORD
     and to seek him in his temple.
For in the day of trouble
     he will keep me safe in his dwelling;
he will hide me in the shelter of his sacred tent
     and set me high upon a rock (Psalm 27:1, 3–5).

What key insight stands out to you from this passage?

How does the psalmist react to the fears that he is facing?

WATCH

Play the video segment for session four. As you watch, fill in the blanks in the following outline and also record any thoughts or concepts that stand out to you.

NOTES

We will face situations that cause us to fear as we do what God has called us to do. We have to take back our lives from fear and stand against those things that cause us fear.

God's calling is for us to lead lives of reckless abandon and wild trust in him. So there will be times when we are going to feel we are in over our heads.

The Bible is filled with exhortations to "fear not," but that doesn't mean we will never feel fear. Rather, the command is to act as bold as a lion even when we are feeling afraid.

Gideon was a man who was initially given over to his fears. God called out the greatness inside of him—a greatness that he himself didn't even know was there.

In God's economy, we will always be outgunned and out-manned—but always on the winning team. God loves to stack the deck against us so that he gets all the glory.

Fear is not from God. It's an opposition trying to pull us back from his call. Given this, we don't have to hold on to our fears—we don't have to choose to believe that spirit of fear.

The trumpet, pitcher, and torch provide us with three take-aways from Gideon's story:

The call of the *trumpet* represents our unity.

The broken *pitcher* represents our availability.

The lit *torch* represents our opportunity in this world.

We have to allow the hard things we've been through to serve as opportunities to let the light shine out of the cracks of the broken places in our heart.

DISCUSS

Take a few minutes with your group members to discuss what you just watched and explore these concepts together.

1. Why do you think God calls us into situations in which we will naturally feel fear?

2. Read Judges 6:11–12. What was Gideon doing when he was visited by the angel of the Lord? How did God call out the warrior within him?

3. Read 2 Timothy 1:7. What does the apostle Paul say about fear in this verse? What does he encourage you to remember when you feel fear?

4. How did Gideon come to understand that the battle would not come by relying on his own strength but only by trusting in God's greater plan?

5. How have you seen God use stressful situations to build unity in the church?

6. How is God calling you to be available and take risks for him today?

RESPOND

Briefly review the outline for the video teaching and any notes you took. In the space below, write down the most significant point you took away from this session.

PRAY

Wrap up your time together by taking a few minutes to talk with God. Here are a few ideas of what you could pray about based on what you discussed in this session:

- Ask God to reveal how he wants to use your life for his purposes.
- Pray for the courage to not walk in fear but in the freedom to follow God's call.
- Thank God for the people who encourage you, for the strength that he gives you, and for the opportunities to serve him.
- Declare that fear has no hold on you as you resolve to keep your eyes fixed on God's promise to be with you.

BETWEEN-SESSIONS PERSONAL STUDY

Before you begin this personal study, you may want to review week 4 in *Take Back Your Life*. Be sure to also read the reflection questions after each activity and make a few notes in your guide about the experience. Once again, there will be a few minutes for you to share any insights you learned at the start of the next session.

Day 22

HHT HHT HHT HHT II

THE NEAREST LION

Though a host encamp against me,
my heart will not fear; though war arise against me,
in spite of this I shall be confident.

Psalm 27:3 NASB

I am fascinated by the way lions hunt. I've read that it is the lionesses that actually do the "lion's share" of the work. The males are obviously incredibly intimidating, with their manes and their ferocious roars. But the fact that lionesses do not have this recognizable mane actually helps them to sneak up on whatever they are hunting.

The males do play a small role in the hunt. Here is how it works. As the females stalk their prey from behind, the king of the jungle will come from the front and let loose a roar so loud it can be heard for up to five miles away. When the gazelle, antelope, or other prey hear the terrifying noise, they turn and run away from the sound.

What these poor creatures don't realize is that the one who did the roaring is more bark than bite. So away they go . . . *directly into the path of the waiting lionesses.* In other words, the prey's instincts are all wrong. Going with their gut causes them to make the wrong choice.

It's shocking how often that is true in our lives as well. When we run from things that scare us, we end up moving *toward* the danger, not away from it. If we fail to face our fears, they will always be waiting right there behind us.

It's counterintuitive, but's true. So, when you feel that panicky fight-or-flight sensation, and you want to run away, do just the opposite. Run *toward* the roar.

✖ What do you find most challenging about God's invitation to remain confident and fearless in him when you are faced with challenging situations?

✖ What fear have you been running from rather than face? How has that approach worked for you?

✖ Now imagine running toward the roar. What would it look like if you remained confident and fearless as you confronted those situations head-on with God?

Day 23

||||| |||| ||||| |||| |||

LET IT GO

I consider that the sufferings of this present time
are not worth comparing with the glory
that is to be revealed to us.

Romans 8:18 RSV

Fear of failure can keep us in the shallows of life. We want to launch out bravely into the great unknown. But we worry we'll blow it, and so we come back to shore hanging our heads.

Know this: not only is failure not a bad thing, but it is also a *necessary* thing. The only way to get to victory is by being willing to make mistakes on the way there. True overnight successes are rare. Far more often, we have to keep showing up, day in and day out, until the hard, unglamorous work adds up and pays off.

It's easy to overlook this fact when you see successful people taking a victory lap. But know this celebration represents only the tip of the iceberg. Invisible to your eye is what is under the surface—all the pain and struggle they endured on the road to that success.

Often, running toward the roar isn't about something we're supposed to do but something we have to go through. I have experienced this in my own life. But I have also found that God was there with me through the flashbacks, the sleepless nights, the tears, and the lack of tears. He will be with you as well, as you go through your times of pain.

A wise person once observed that most people die at twenty-five and aren't buried until they're seventy-five. Don't let that happen to you. All that's holding you back? *Let it go.* And then choose instead to believe the day is coming when what you are most scared of right now will be included in your highlight reel as a victory.

✗ What do you perceive as your greatest failure right now? Why?

✗ Do you tend to give yourself grace when you don't do things perfectly—or punish yourself for making mistakes? Where do you think this negative response originated?

✗ How might you take what you're most scared of now and turn it into a future victory?

Day 24

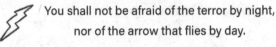

TERROR BY NIGHT

You shall not be afraid of the terror by night,
nor of the arrow that flies by day.

Psalm 91:5 NKJV

God promises in his Word that if we make him our God, we do not have to be afraid of any terrors in the night. As someone who has struggled with fear my whole life, I find this very comforting. But it's important for us to remember that just because God says we don't have to fear evil doesn't mean that we will never feel afraid.

Protection isn't the same as exemption. Following Jesus doesn't put us in a luxury box seat. We are going to be in the thick of it, our face marred by dust and sweat and grime as we charge headlong into action, knowing that God both goes before us and stands as our rear guard. Following God means being on the front lines of a battle and knowing that he has got our back.

We can see how this played out in Jesus' life. God brought him safely through the battles he faced—including death—but that didn't mean he was never attacked. In fact, his public ministry was bookended by two extreme battles with fear: the temptation in the wilderness and his suffering in the Garden of Gethsemane. If God didn't spare his own Son from attacks, we can be assured that we will face trials in this life as well.

So, the next time you experience terror by night, remember the greatest human being who ever lived did too. But he also reveals that when you choose to "abide under the shadow of the Almighty," that terror cannot touch you. You can rest in that truth tonight.

✗ What currently represents the "terror by night" in your life?

✗ How has God proven to you that he has "got your back" in the battle?

✗ How has God guided you through trying times when you chose to abide in him?

Day 25

卌 卌 卌 卌 卌

A TRIP TO THE DUMP

 If we confess our sins to him, he is faithful and just to forgive us our sins and to cleanse us from all wickedness.

1 John 1:9 NLT

One year, I challenged our church to do a seven-day fast so that we could recenter our hearts on heaven. I decided to take the week off not just from food but from buying anything online. It was honestly more challenging than giving up food! I hadn't realized how compulsive my online shopping had become, even though we had a garage filled with empty Amazon boxes.

The day I could no longer get into the garage, I decided to do something about it. I put on an audiobook, grabbed a box cutter, and went to work cutting them down. I filled up every square inch of my SUV and took the boxes to the giant recycling receptacle at the dump.

The truth is we all need to undergo a similar kind of purge on the inside—*regularly*. We accumulate gunk, grime, and shame in our hearts and minds just from being alive. We need an outlet for all that junk. This is why regular confession is such an important part of our relationship with God. As we sin, are hurt, get offended, and offend others, the garages of our hearts get filled with trash and boxes and hurt feelings and regrets.

Without a regular purge, your soul will quickly become overrun with the stinking thinking and rotting feelings that accumulate over time—things like fears, discouragement, anger, and jealousy. So, it's time to come clean. And the only way to come clean is to bare your heart before the Lord. In essence, it is a trip to the dump for your soul.

✗ What effect does carrying around hurt feelings and regret have on your attitude and relationships?

✗ When is the last time you had a purge on the inside—getting rid of all the gunk, grime, and shame in your heart and mind?

✗ Is confession of your sins a daily spiritual practice for you? Why or why not?

Day 26

~~HHT~~ ~~HHT~~ ~~HHT~~ ~~HHT~~ ~~HHT~~ I

USE WHAT YOU'VE GOT

His divine power has given us everything we need
for a godly life through our knowledge of him
who called us by his own glory and goodness.

2 Peter 1:3

A gym membership can be a great tool in helping you get in shape. It will give you access to go into a facility that has all kinds of machines you can use to work out muscles, build up strength, and reduce body fat. But just because you have the right to go to the gym and freely use the equipment doesn't automatically mean you get a six-pack. You actually have to walk in and take advantage of what your gym membership provides.

The same is true when it comes to the arsenal of power that you have at your beck and call as a child of God. The power that leads to victory is not in you or from you. Rather, it is with God and comes to you from his hand. It is available to you! As Peter states, you have "all things that pertain to life and godliness." But that power has to be *wielded*. Like a gym membership, you actually have to take advantage of what you have been given for it to be effective.

One of the biggest mistakes that you can make is to try to do God's work without God's power. So many Christians today try to fight the battles of this life with their own strength, waging war according to the flesh. Don't make that same error! Jesus is not something to carry around like a religious trinket or a good-luck charm. He is the risen Lord who will carry you and cause the ground to shake with energy.

The name of Jesus—not just a generic God or the man upstairs—is what gives you power. It's completely available to you. All you need to do is *use what you've got.*

✗ Why do you think so many Christians go through life with the misguided belief that God gave them brains and strength—so now it's up to them to make things happen?

✗ When have you tried to do God's work without God's power? What were the results?

✗ In what areas of your life do you need to "use what you've got" when it comes to tapping into God's incredible power?

𝍷𝍷𝍷𝍷 𝍷𝍷𝍷𝍷 𝍷𝍷𝍷𝍷 𝍷𝍷𝍷𝍷 𝍷𝍷𝍷𝍷 𝍷𝍷

THE BEST DEFENSE IS A GOOD OFFENSE

 The reason the Son of God appeared
was to destroy the devil's work.

1 John 3:8

When you begin to get your heart right, don't be surprised if the devil doubles down. The enemy of your soul gets nervous when he sees good things happen. So he lets out a roar. But know this: when the devil starts to mess with you, it's a mistake on his part. Every time he fights against something, he tips his hand so you can see what matters to him.

The only reason the enemy comes against you is because he sees value in you. It's because you are precious to God that he tries to make you feel worthless to everyone else. It's because you are meant to choose life that he would suggest you should choose death. Whatever he says, you can know the opposite is true, because he is a liar.

The devil opposes whatever causes him to fear. So, let your fear help you sniff out what he is trying to snuff out. Let it be a diagnostic tool to determine your calling. And then . . . *run toward the roar*! Rise up and do exactly what the devil doesn't want you to do. Refuse to go gently into the night. Don't be taken without a fight.

In jujitsu, you use your opponent's force and energy against him. Likewise, when you experience terror during the darkness, become a source of terror to the kingdom of darkness. Practice terror-jitsu and remember . . . *the best defense is a good offense.*

✗ John writes that Jesus came to destroy the devil's work. How would you describe the work that Jesus is destroying? Why is that destruction so essential?

✗ Where is the enemy currently tipping his hand in your life? How might that serve as a diagnostic tool to clarify your calling?

✗ In jujitsu, you use the enemy's energy and force against him. In what way can you rise up and do exactly what the devil doesn't want you to do?

Day 28

HtH HtH HtH HtH HtH |||

HOPE HAS A ROPE

> We have this hope as an anchor for the soul, firm and secure.
> It enters the inner sanctuary behind the curtain, where our
> forerunner, Jesus, has entered on our behalf.
>
> Hebrews 6:19–20

My wife, Jennie, and I both have anchor tattoos. The symbol of the anchor is powerful because of what it stands for: *hope*. And hope is a powerful thing.

At its most basic level, to have hope is to believe that something good is going to happen. It is to trust that help is on its way and everything is not over yet. It means that no matter how dark it seems, there is going to be light at the end of the tunnel. Our hope is a living hope, because we have a living Lord. It is "an anchor for the soul" (Hebrews 6:19).

However, for anchors to be effective, they have to be attached to a rope or a chain. That connection is every bit as vital as the anchor itself. After all, it doesn't matter how securely that big hunk of metal might be wedged to the ocean floor if there is nothing connecting it to the boat. If the boat is not tied to it, it won't be the least bit helpful to sailors onboard.

The wonderful thing about the anchor of our soul is that it, too, comes equipped with a mighty chain: the Holy Spirit. Before entering God's presence in the ascension, Jesus promised to send his Spirit to be our helper (see John 14:15–31). He is our great rope that cannot be frayed—the one who has lashed our hearts to heaven. He is the proof that there is more in store and that death is not the end.

In times of overwhelming fear or darkness and weariness from fighting, your *anchor* should strengthen you, but you should also be encouraged by the *chain*. Remember that *hope has a rope*. Keep your anchor on a short leash, and when fearful times come, you'll have the strength to move forward without being lost at sea.

- How have you witnessed the power of hope recently in your life?

- In what area of your life have you been losing hope recently? Can you describe what has led to this sense of hopelessness?

- The anchor of the soul comes equipped with a strong rope—the Holy Spirit. In what ways might remembering this strengthen your relationship with the Holy Spirit?

For Next Week: Use the space on the following page to write down any insights or questions that you want to discuss at the next group meeting. In preparation for next week, review weeks 5 and 6 in *Take Back Your Life*.

EMBRACE THE STRUGGLE

The harder the conflict, the more glorious the triumph.
What we obtain too cheap, we esteem too lightly;
it is dearness only that gives everything its value.

Thomas Paine

WELCOME

By the time Clara Barton founded the American Red Cross in 1881, a lifetime of service had taught her the value of embracing struggles and persevering through trials. As a young child, she was so painfully shy that she is only known to have one friend. This timidity continued well into her high school years. Eventually, her parents persuaded her to become a schoolteacher to boost her confidence, and she found great success in this profession.

By 1852, her reputation led to her securing a contract to open a school in New Jersey. Her accomplishments compelled the town to raise $4,000 for a new school building. However, once the school was opened, Clara was replaced as its principal. The board members saw the position as the head of a large institution to be "unfitting" for a woman. The setback caused Clara to suffer a nervous breakdown and other health issues.

By 1855, she had taken a job in the U.S. Patent Office, where she suffered much abuse at the hands of her male counterparts. It wasn't until the outbreak of the Civil War in 1861 that Clara stepped into the position that would define the rest of her life, when she began volunteering to care for wounded soldiers. Her skills eventually led her to the battlefield, where she often had to make do without proper supplies and was frequently put in harm's way.

At the end of the war, Clara again endured ridicule when she embraced the woman's suffrage movement and became an activist for civil rights. The stress caused her to fall ill and forced her to take a break from the work she was doing. Down but never out, she continued to embrace her struggles and became stronger because of them. By 1878, she was

meeting with U.S. presidents and arguing for the establish-
ment of a unified organization that could respond to crises
in the country. Her efforts ultimately led to the foundation
of the American Red Cross.

In our own lives, we will encounter days, months, and
even years when everything just seems to be a challenge.
How we choose to respond to these "wilderness times" will
shape the rest of our lives. For as we will see in this final
session, God will use these challenges to prepare us for his
work. In the end, we find that we are stronger as a result of
everything we have endured.

SHARE

Begin your group time by inviting those in the group to
share their insights from last week's personal study. Then,
to kick things off, discuss one of the following questions:

- How you would define "wilderness times" in your
  own life?

  — *or* —

- How have you witnessed the value of persevering
  through trials?

READ

Invite someone to read aloud the following passage. Listen
for fresh insights as you hear the verses being read, and then
discuss the questions that follow.

Very early in the morning, while it was still dark, Jesus got up, left the house and went off to a solitary place, where he prayed. Simon and his companions went to look for him, and when they found him, they exclaimed: "Everyone is looking for you!" Jesus replied, "Let us go somewhere else—to the nearby villages—so I can preach there also. That is why I have come." So he traveled throughout Galilee, preaching in their synagogues and driving out demons (Mark 1:35–39).

What key insight stands out to you from this passage?

What does this passage reveal about the way that Jesus prepared for ministry?

WATCH

Play the video segment for session five. As you watch, fill in the blanks in the following outline and also record any thoughts or concepts that stand out to you.

NOTES

We are entering into a new period of testing and must struggle our way through. Like a butterfly in a cocoon, it's the struggle that will teach us how to fly.

God's will for our lives is more journey than destination—more about the process than the arrival. The key is to keep moving forward and embracing changes in times of uncertainty.

Jesus provides a template on what it means to find a rhythm for our soul and be in a place of health—body, spirit, mind, heart, soul, and strength. We find in the stories of his early ministry:

Jesus follows God's plan and the Holy Spirit descends on him like a dove.

The Holy Spirit leads Jesus into the wilderness, where he is tested.

Jesus delighted in the wilderness and saw it as a source of strength.

We're living in a day where wilderness and solitude—being alone and being quiet enough to hear from heaven—is a rare commodity. The world has changed . . . and changed *a lot*.

We have tools at our disposal that allow us to communicate all the time with people everywhere. But it's a double-edged sword that comes with good *and* bad implications.

It's important to follow Jesus' example and take time to be in solitude and immersed in quiet. There are three practical ways that we can incorporate this into our lives:

Be in motion—just enjoy the idea of walking with God.

Be in nature—allow it to spark your "God-ward" thoughts.

Be in silence—take time to settle and soothe your soul.

Take control of what you can. Go into this new season strong because of what God gives you in the secret place. You will see him do something powerful in your life.

DISCUSS

Take a few minutes with your group members to discuss what you just watched and explore these concepts together.

1. How is struggle part of the process of finding success and victory in life?

2. Read Mark 1:12–13 and Matthew 14:22–23. How did Jesus use time in the wilderness to connect with God? How did this time prepare him to fulfill God's purposes?

3. What are some of the struggles that you encounter in finding time alone with God? Why is it important to make this time a priority in your day?

4. Jesus was *in motion* and walked everywhere he went. How can you incorporate this practice of being in motion into your time with God?

5. Jesus was *in nature* and actually with the beasts during his forty days in the wilderness. How can you incorporate this practice of being in nature into your time with God?

6. Jesus was intentional about being *in silence* with God. How can you likewise be intentional about spending time in silence before God?

RESPOND

Briefly review the outline for the video teaching and any notes you took. In the space below, write down the most significant point you took away from this session.

PRAY

Wrap up your time together by taking a few minutes to talk with God. Here are a few ideas of what you could pray about based on what you discussed in this session:

- Ask God to help you embrace the struggle to make time with him a priority.
- Pray for the wisdom and strength to use your time with God wisely.
- Ask God to help you find ways to be in motion, in nature, and in silence in the times you spend with him each day.
- Declare that you are committed to spending regular quiet time with God as you move forward in obedience to his plan for your life.

BETWEEN-SESSIONS PERSONAL STUDY

Before you begin this final personal study, you may want to review weeks 5 and 6 in *Take Back Your Life.* Be sure to also read the reflection questions after each activity and make a few notes in your guide about the experience. Consider sharing these insights with your group members in the days and weeks following the conclusion of this study.

Day 29

~~卌~~ ~~卌~~ ~~卌~~ ~~卌~~ ~~卌~~ ||||

STAY IN THE PACK

Just as each of us has one body with many members, and these members do not all have the same function, so in Christ we, though many, form one body, and each member belongs to all the others.

Romans 12:4–5

You need people in your life as you seek to *take back your life*. God never intended for this journey to be a solo act. You were made for community.

Take a cue here from the wolves. Many people don't realize it, but wolves are social creatures. Every wolf has a pack. They care for their pups with devotion. They hold a place in their society for the elders. They care for one another, miss each other when they are separated, and grieve when a member of the pack dies.

This wolf pack—a protective and organized force of nature—is part of your destiny. Simply put, you were meant to do life with others. And life is better together.

So, the question becomes, *Who are the people in your pack?* Who are the people with whom you are doing life? Give serious thought to this, because it's been said you are the average of the five people with whom you are the closest. It only makes sense if you're going to do life with people, you are going to end up where they are going.

It's nearly impossible to live a fulfilled life on your own. Being part of the pack is not just a gift but also a necessity.

To make a difference in this world, to live your story, you're going to need your pack beside you. So, make sure you choose your pack members well.

✗ Whether you consider yourself introverted or extroverted, do you agree that God designed people to need community? Why or why not?

✗ Who (other than your family) are in your pack? In what ways do you regularly pour into them with your unique personality and talent?

✗ How have you seen your life benefit from the people you've chosen to be in your pack?

Day 30

HHT THL HHT THL HHT THL

THE POWER OF THE HOWL

 Encourage one another and build each other up,
just as in fact you are doing.

1 Thessalonians 5:11

What makes a wolf pack work? What bonds them all together and allows them to function as a team? What keeps them healthy and alive? It's all about communication.

When you think of the way in which wolves communicate, perhaps that bone-chilling howl they are so famous for immediately comes to mind. But did you know they purposely avoid harmonizing when howling? Wolves howl with their own unique pitch so they can appear more numerous than they are. They're pitchy on purpose.

But the howling is just one way they communicate. They also stay united through facial expressions, scent, body language, and touching. In the same way, experts estimate that only a small percent of our communication occurs through words. The great majority of what we say each day involves what we do with our bodies, our facial expressions, and our tone. Of course, this can be problematic when most of our communication occurs via text and email!

God loves the people in your life so much that he put *you* in their lives. And he gave you the means to communicate with them so they could be better off because they encountered you. So, consider the words that you are saying to them—and what you are communicating to them through your body language. Remember the *power of the howl* when it comes to running with the members of your pack.

✗ Is it easy for you to share your feelings and ideas with others? Why or why not?

✗ Are you aware of how much you communicate nonverbally? When you aren't engaged or present to others around you, how does that play out in your body language?

✗ What are some things you can do or say today to build up and encourage the members of your pack?

Day 31

~~HHT~~ ~~HHT~~ ~~HHT~~ ~~HHT~~ ~~HHT~~ ~~HHT~~ |

DON'T KICK THE BEEHIVE

There is one who speaks rashly like the thrusts of a sword,
but the tongue of the wise brings healing.

Proverbs 12:18 NASB

Dale Carnegie said, "If you want to gather honey, don't kick over the beehive." Think about this statement for a moment. If a bee stings you while you're gathering honey, kicking the beehive will only make the situation worse. Rather, "a gentle answer turns away wrath" and will help you get what you want (Proverbs 15:1). This is why beekeepers use slow movements (and smoke cans) to calm the bees before they try to take the honey from the hive.

Studies reveal that rudeness causes performance issues and a decline in spirit on a team. It impacts creativity and drive. Being rude is not just cheap but also expensive. And you don't even have to be the recipient of the rude behavior. Simply *witnessing* incivility brings negative consequences.

Deep down, you know this. Even while you are sassing your parents, being sarcastic with your spouse, or spouting off at the rude customer service person, you know you are making the problem worse. But in those moments, you don't care. You just want to kick the beehive.

The difference between people and animals (and yes, even wolves) is that, because you were made in the image of God, you can choose to *not* just react on what you feel. You can choose something better. You can choose something in line with your calling, your identity, and your greater purpose toward others. You can back up your good intentions with solid actions.

So don't kick the beehive, for your own good . . . and for the good of the pack.

✘ When have you recently given into your frustrations and "kicked over the beehive"?

✘ It's a hard lesson to learn—but you can choose not to do what you feel when you are irritated. What is an example of you making this better choice? What was the result?

✘ Words can cut as easily as they can heal. Who needs your healing words today? What are some ways you need to make amends for using cutting words?

Day 32

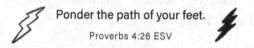

FOUR SQUARES FOR A BETTER YOU

Ponder the path of your feet.

Proverbs 4:26 ESV

Our culture places a high value on being true to ourselves. Not doing and saying what we feel is hard because it flies in the face of that concept. But consider this: carefully choosing your words and responses leads to something even better—becoming who you want to be.

With this in mind, I've come up with a four-part matrix that can help you manage yourself when things get dicey with others. It's a model based on the words of Proverbs 4:26. It involves pondering the path of your feet rather than putting your feet in your mouth!

To begin, draw a cross. In the top quadrants, from left to right, put the words *analyze* and *extrapolate*. In the bottom quadrants, write *prioritize* and *navigate*.

Under *analyze*, write, "*I want to . . .*" and then write exactly what you want to say or do because you are angry, sad, or rejected. Don't fight it. Just feel it. Under *extrapolate*, write, "*If I do this, then this will happen.*" Play out the scenario to its logical end. It can be incredibly helpful to understand the implications of a decision before taking action.

Moving to the lower quadrants, under *prioritize*, write, "*What I really want to happen is . . .*" In other words, if you were to come up with the storyboard for this situation, what would be the final scene before the credits started to roll? Finally, under *navigate*, write, *"What I need to do to get there is . . ."* Write it down. Remember that it will often be the opposite of whatever you originally felt like doing.

And there you have it. Four squares for a better you.

✘ Consider a situation in which you are struggling to control your words and actions. In the chart below, answer the questions in the four quadrants.

ANALYZE:	EXTRAPOLATE:
What do you want to do?	*What will happen if you do this?*
PRIORITIZE:	**NAVIGATE:**
What do you really want to happen?	*What do you need to do to get there?*

✘ How can this exercise better help you to "ponder the path of your feet" (Proverbs 4:26)?

ʰ**Ⅲ** ʰ**Ⅲ** ʰ**Ⅲ** ʰ**Ⅲ** ʰ**Ⅲ** ʰ**Ⅲ** Ⅲ

RISE HIGH, BOW LOW

 You're sons of Light, daughters of Day. . . .
Since we're creatures of Day, let's act like it.

1 Thessalonians 5:4–8 MSG

Researchers have found that a wolf pack has a social structure and rules of conduct. The pack leaders are called the *alphas*. These two animals—male and female—are dominant over the other wolves in the pack. (Scientists can actually tell which wolves will fulfill this role based on how they carry themselves as pups.) Then there are the *omega* wolves, who are at the bottom of the pecking order. Yet researchers have found they are undeniably loved by the pack.

Here's something that blew my mind. When wolves enter a den, they slide in on their bellies through the hole and do a bow before the alphas. Apparently, it is an honor thing. If the wolf served in the military, the bow would be the equivalent of a salute with respect. And no wolf in the entire pack bows lower than the omega. The omega wolf bows the lowest of all.

When I consider this, I think about Jesus, who said, "I am the Alpha and the Omega. I'm the first and the last. I'm the one who was and is. I am the Lord almighty" (Revelation 1:8, my paraphrase). Jesus was the *alpha* of all, but he lowered himself to become human. And not just any human, but an *omega*, the lowest of all. As a servant, he died even the death of the cross.

My encouragement to you, as an individual and in your pack, is to live a life bowing low before Jesus, the Alpha and the Omega. You can realize so much power when you get your posture right—when you let your life be marked by worship and surrender to God. Bowing down low before Jesus puts you in a position where God can cause you to rise high.

✗ Whether in family, work, church, or politics, it's rare for the most powerful individual to humble themselves before those with less power. Why do you think this is the case?

✗ How did Jesus prove through his life, death, and resurrection that he is both the Alpha and the Omega? How does that reality impact your life?

✗ Bowing down makes you poised to rise up. In what area of your life could you benefit from "bowing" more? What is a practical way you could begin doing this now?

Day 34

HHT THL HHT THL HHT THL IIII

TWO STEPS TO THE LEFT

 Not by might, nor by power, but by My Spirit,
says the Lord of hosts.

Zechariah 4:6 ESV

As I mentioned in this week's session, I like to be in motion and be in nature when spending time with God. I find I pray better walking. I think better walking. It's just rejuvenating to my spirit. I get to zone out and just stroll.

There is one path in particular that I frequent. I was on this trail one day when I noticed I was walking in a strange fashion, almost like I was playing hopscotch. I realized I was trying to avoid all the little gifts that had been left by a flock of Canada geese. The amount of poop was insane that day. There was almost no exposed pavement.

Yet I persisted. Let it never be said that a Canada goose ever got the best of me. I finally got to the end, only to realize I had to turn around and do it all over again. It was then I looked to my left and saw a grassy belt running parallel to the path. It was completely clean and open. I took two steps to my left, and from then on it was poop-free all the way home.

I think this illustrates the difference between trying to live for God and letting God's life live through you. Maybe you're at your wit's end in your marriage. Or on your last nerve with your kids? Or running on empty at work? If so, just ask the Holy Spirit to shift you two steps to the left.

Perhaps like me on my walk, you'll go from awkward flailing to smooth sailing.

God has the power. You just need to ask for it. Then let him reveal where in your life you need to take just two steps to the left.

✗ It's easy to fall into the pattern of doing the same things the same way every day. What are some areas where you might be in a rut?

✗ How could you get out of this rut if you took just "two steps to the left"?

✗ What does it mean to live by God's Spirit rather than your own might and power?

Day 35

卌 卌 卌 卌 卌 卌 卌

PENCILS DOWN

 You do not even know what will happen tomorrow.
What is your life? You are a mist that appears for
a little while and then vanishes.

James 4:14

I can't think of any two words I associate with a terrible feeling in the pit of my stomach more than the phrase, "pencils down." It is the sound of a hundred tests I wasn't prepared for. When I heard these words, I would tear through the remaining questions, filling in as many bubbles as I could: C, C, C, C, C, C, C, C . . . I figured one out of four was better odds than zero out of four.

Here's the truth of it: *life is a timed test*. You're living against a deadline. The Bible says that a moment is coming when God will say "pencils down" to each you. "It is appointed for men to die once, and after that comes judgment" (Hebrews 9:27 ESV). You have a limited amount of time to act on the plans God has for you. No pressure, but anything you don't tap into by the time this life ends shall remain undone forever.

As James writes, life is like a mist. It is true for you, those you love, and those you are meant to impact. Live each day all the way to the hilt, because each day could be your final one here. There is a hereafter, and when you leave this world, you will get to go to your true home. But the way you live here will have an impact on what you experience when you arrive there.

A thousand years from now, you won't be able to change what you did during your lifetime. But if you do it right, you will be enjoying the fruits from it. In the words of Maximus Decimus Meridius from *Gladiator*, "What we do in life echoes in eternity."

✘ Are you comforted or concerned by the words, "You do not even know what will happen tomorrow" (James 4:14)? Why does an unknown future provoke that response in you?

✘ You have a limited amount of time to act on the plans God has for you. What three things do you most want to accomplish before you hear the phrase "pencils down"?

✘ How do you think the three items you listed will one day "echo in eternity"?

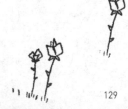

KEEP GOING!

Complete your forty-day interactive journey to *taking back your life* by completing the following readings for days 36 to 40. Use the questions provided to help you go deeper into each day's theme. Thank you for your commitment to "embrace the struggle" and persevere in this study!

Day 36

HHT THL HHT THL HHT THL HHT I

KEEP FIGHTING

 Delight yourself in the Lᴏʀᴅ,
and he will give you the desires of your heart.

Psalm 37:4 ESV

Think about a butterfly in its cocoon. If you cut it out or help it out in any way, it will never develop the strength it needs in its wings to be able to achieve take-off. Butterflies have to struggle out in order to come into their own. Flight only comes after the fight.

The same goes for your calling. You're destined for impact. You're beloved by God. You are unspeakably valuable. You were made by God for his joy and for his grand purpose. But you may be wondering what your next step should be. If you're struggling with that question, I say, "Good!" Keep struggling. Keep wrestling with it. Keep showing up every day and fighting. You will come out of it with stronger wings.

We often treat the subject of God's will as though it were this crazy, exotic, strange mystery. But in truth, it's far less cryptic. *God's calling for your life is more about who you are becoming than where you are going.* It's less about what you do and more about how well you do whatever you do. It's not something you sit around and wait to receive but something that is all around you. It's here and ready, if you just take the first step to break from the cocoon.

God goes before you and sets things up. He guides you in his providence and prepares things for you to discover. But these are things you can't see in the mirror right now. You can't see them until you look back. So just believe they will be there as you keep fighting!

✖ What does it mean to "delight yourself in the LORD" (Psalm 37:4)? How might you pursue that on a regular basis?

✖ It's our nature to avoid struggle, but the struggle is actually crucial for us. In your life, where have you seen the truth of the idea that "flight only comes after the fight"?

✖ What is an example of a time when God went before you and prepared things in ways you couldn't have anticipated until after the fact?

Day 37

IIII IIII IIII IIII IIII IIII IIII II

STAND ON TIPTOES

 For the earnest expectation of the creation eagerly waits
for the revealing of the sons of God.

Romans 8:19 NKJV

If you're discouraged by the difference between who you are now and who you want to be, think of it this way. Today is like Saturday. Between Jesus' burial on Friday and his resurrection on Sunday, there was Saturday. Good Friday is famous and Easter Sunday is awesome, but in between, there is this day that doesn't get a lot of play.

We are living in the spirit of an extended Saturday. We have a living Savior, so we have a living hope. We know we can make it through our Saturday because God has promised to bring us to Sunday. The trouble is we have no idea when our Saturday will end. Jesus told us that no one but his Father knows the date of his return, and none of us knows for certain when our day will come to die. So we have to just trust that Sunday is on its way.

In the meantime, we wait in "earnest expectation" for that day. The term Paul used literally means "to stand on your tiptoes and crane your neck." Paul is saying the whole world is so full of edge-of-your-seat excitement concerning the return of Jesus and the glory that will be unleashed that it can't contain itself from being on tiptoes in anticipation.

The future is where you must focus, not the past. When your heart is focused on the things that are to come instead of paralyzed by the hard and the horrible things you've had to handle, you are postured to be effective in the present.

You have to make the choice to live on your spiritual tiptoes, setting your mind on things above, not on things of this earth. To the degree that you cultivate your sense of longing for the next world, you'll be able to combat the deadly hypnotizing pull of this one and the downward spiral that happens when you look around instead of up.

✕ How do you describe the gap between where you are now and where you want to be?

✕ Why is it important for you to focus on the future rather than the past?

✕ How does setting your mind on things above rather than of this earth help you be more effective here in the present?

Day 38

|||| |||| |||| |||| |||| |||| |||| |||

NEVER BRING A HORSE
TO A TANK FIGHT

You will receive power when the Holy Spirit comes on you;
and you will be my witnesses in Jerusalem,
and in all Judea and Samaria, and to the ends of the earth.

Acts 1:8

We are just about at the end of our time together. And if you're still with me—if you've soldiered your way to this final week—then it means you are serious about bettering yourself. In that, if you've declared war on the version of your life you don't want to live, the version of yourself you don't want to be, you've crossed the barbed wire. There's no going back now!

But now that you've reached this point, please remember that *it isn't all up to you.* You've got something at your disposal far more powerful than self-help. You've got God's help. And, frankly, without that help . . . you're basically toast.

Think of it in terms of riding out to do battle against a tank on horseback. This is actually what occurred in the early days of World War I, when fighting techniques were evolving from traditional cavalry units to mechanized war machines. It also happened in the battles following 9/11, when al-Qaeda hunkered down in the mountains of Afghanistan.

As depicted in the movie *12 Strong*, the most jaw-dropping scene took place when the soldiers charged onto the battlefield against machine-gun-laden pickup trucks and even full-blown tanks. The Americans would have been doomed if that were the end of the story, but they also had a laser pointer and a satellite phone. With those two vital pieces of equipment, they were able to call for fire to rain from the sky.

It wasn't what the soldiers brought into the battle that made them dangerous but who was on the other end of the phone—the most powerful military in the history of humankind. We are likewise not to wage war according to our own resources. The power that leads to victory is not in us or from us. It is with God and comes to us from his hand.

x Do you sometimes believe the lie that facing your struggles is all up to you? Why is God-help the ultimate rescue from self-help?

x How have you witnessed "fire rain from the sky" when you have asked God for help?

x How does embracing the truth that all power comes from the Holy Spirit take the pressure off you to come through and make things happen?

Day 39

FIGHT THE FEAR

My weapons have the power of God to destroy the camps
of the enemy. I destroy every claim and every reason that
keeps people from knowing God. I keep every thought
under control in order to make it obey Christ.

2 Corinthians 10:4–5 NIRV

For many people, anxiety and worry seem to be the new normal. Where peace used to exist, only fear and anxiety now thrive. We need to fight the fear instead of feeding it.

As Paul said to the believers in Corinth, the devil wants the high ground in our lives so he can shoot down on us. To keep that from happening, we have to hold the high ground by taking control of our hearts, our emotions, and our minds. These represent the theater of war.

Worship, prayer, and Scripture reading will give us that high ground. The supernatural power of God gives us our strength, and we can't fight without connecting to him. But I think even little, boring, everyday things are important too. Like sleep . . . get eight hours a night. And hydration . . . drink eight glasses of water a day. And what you start and end your day with . . give the first and last eight minutes of every day over to Jesus. Remember it this way: 8-8-8.

As you do these little things in life, it will serve to starve your fear and feed your faith. It will help you to recognize there is way too much God wants to do in your life right now to give one more second over to fear, worry, narcissism, loneliness, and all the other things that cause wheels to spin and darkness to grow. Once you've declared war, your mentality will shift.

These are not peacetime conditions. So live smarter and make smarter choices on a day-to-day basis. Hold the high ground by fighting your fears instead of feeding them.

✖ Has your level of fear or worry increased recently? If so, what seems to be fueling it?

✖ How does remembering that you have an enemy and are not in peacetime conditions help in your fight against fear?

✖ What are some specific ways you are fighting your fears instead of feeding them?

Day 40

‖‖ ‖‖ ‖‖ ‖‖ ‖‖ ‖‖ ‖‖ ‖‖

GET UP AND SHOW UP

 Blessed is a man who perseveres under trial; for once he has
been approved, he will receive the crown of life
which the Lord has promised to those who love Him.

James 1:12 NASB

As we come to the end of our study, I want to ask where you are in your journey. What are you thinking about quitting? What dream are you beginning to lose faith in?

Here's the truth: *this is a fight.* It's not just one round and it's over. It's not just, "Well, there, I fought in the battle. I tried to control my thoughts. I tried to speak differently. I tried to start the business. I tried to work on my marriage. I tried to take back my life." That is not a fight!

A fight is getting knocked down and getting back up again. It's like Rocky Balboa in the movies, who frequently hit the mat but always got back up on his feet. It's like Muhammad Ali using the rope-a-dope technique in the Rumble in the Jungle against heavyweight champion George Foreman. The enemy thinks you're trapped against the ropes, but actually you're just getting started.

A fight is bloody round after bloody round. It's going from failure to failure but choosing to press on. It's also remembering that you are not alone. Yes, winning the war within is difficult, but there are people in your family, people in your life, and people you don't even know yet who are trying to win it too. If you give up, how will God use you to reach them?

As you continue to fight the good fight, know that you are not just fighting for yourself. God wants to save lives through you. Who knows what your legacy will be if you keep getting up and showing up tomorrow and the next day and all the days after that. So, get up and show up—and *take back your life.*

✗ Where do you find it the most difficult to get up and show up in your life? Why do you sense that area is most opposed?

✗ Does it help to remember you aren't alone in this fight? Who else are you passionate about helping to win this war?

✗ We've been on a powerful journey together. What insights or concepts will be the most helpful in this study to take back your life? Why?

LEADER'S GUIDE

Thank you for your willingness to lead your group through this study! What you have chosen to do is valuable and will make a great difference in the lives of others. The rewards of being a leader are different from those of participating, and we hope that as you lead you will find your own walk with Jesus deepened by this experience.

Take Back Your Life is a five-session study built around video content and small-group interaction. As the group leader, just think of yourself as the host of a dinner party. Your job is to take care of your guests by managing all the behind-the-scenes details so that when everyone arrives, they can just enjoy time together.

As the group leader, your role is not to answer all the questions or reteach the content—the video, book, and study guide will do most of that work. Your job is to guide the experience and cultivate your small group into a kind of teaching community. This will make it a place for members to process, question, and reflect—not receive more instruction.

Before your first meeting, make sure everyone in the group gets a copy of the study guide. This will keep everyone on the same page and help the process run more smoothly. If some group members are unable to purchase the guide, arrange it so that people can share the resource with other group members. Giving everyone access to all the material will position this study to be as rewarding an experience as possible. Everyone should feel free to write in his or her study guide and bring it to group every week.

SETTING UP THE GROUP

You will need to determine with your group how long you want to meet each week so you can plan your time accordingly. Generally, most groups like to meet for either ninety minutes or two hours, so you could use one of the following schedules:

SECTION	90 MINUTES	120 MINUTES
WELCOME (members arrive and get settled)	10 minutes	15 minutes
SHARE (discuss one or more of the opening questions for the session)	10 minutes	15 minutes
READ (discuss the questions based on the Scripture reading for the week)	10 minutes	15 minutes
WATCH (watch the teaching material together and take notes)	20 minutes	20 minutes
DISCUSS (discuss the Bible study questions you selected ahead of time)	30 minutes	40 minutes
RESPOND / PRAY (pray together as a group and dismiss)	10 minutes	15 minutes

As the group leader, you'll want to create an environment that encourages sharing and learning. A church sanctuary or formal classroom may not be as ideal as a living room, because those locations can feel formal and less intimate. No matter what setting you choose, provide enough comfortable seating for everyone, and, if possible, arrange the seats in a semicircle so everyone can see the video easily. This will make transition between the video and group conversation more efficient and natural.

Also, try to get to the meeting site early so you can greet participants as they arrive. Simple refreshments create a welcoming atmosphere and can be a wonderful addition to a group study evening. Try to take food and pet allergies into account to make your guests as comfortable as possible. You may also want to consider offering childcare to couples with children who want to attend. Finally, be sure your media technology is working properly. Managing these details up front will make the rest of your group experience flow smoothly and provide a welcoming space in which to engage the content of *Take Back Your Life*.

STARTING THE GROUP TIME

Once everyone has arrived, it's time to begin the group. Here are some simple tips to make your group time healthy, enjoyable, and effective.

First, begin the meeting with a short prayer and remind the group members to put their phones on silent. This is a way to make sure you can all be present with one another and with God. Next, give each person a few minutes to respond to the questions in the "Share" and "Read" sections. This won't require as much time in session one, but beginning in session two, people will need more time to share their insights from their personal studies. Usually, you won't answer the discussion questions yourself, but you should go first with the "Share" and "Read" questions, answering briefly and with a reasonable amount of transparency.

At the end of session one, invite the group members to complete the between-sessions personal studies for that week. Explain that you will be providing some time before the video teaching next week for anyone to share insights. Let them know sharing is optional, and it's no problem if they can't get to some of the between-sessions activities some weeks. It will still be beneficial for them to hear from the other participants and learn about what they discovered.

LEADING THE DISCUSSION TIME

Now that the group is engaged, it's time to watch the video and respond with some directed small-group discussion. Encourage all the group members to participate in the discussion, but make sure they know they don't have to do so. As the discussion progresses, you may want to follow up with comments such as, "Tell me more about that," or, "Why did you answer that way?" This will allow the group participants to deepen their reflections and invite meaningful sharing in a nonthreatening way.

Note that you have been given multiple questions to use in each session, and you do not have to use them all or even follow them in order. Feel free to pick and choose questions based on either the needs of your group or how the conversation is flowing. Also, don't be afraid of silence. Offering a question and allowing up to thirty seconds of silence is okay. It allows people space to think about how they want to respond and also gives them time to do so.

As group leader, you are the boundary keeper for your group. Do not let anyone (yourself included) dominate the group time. Keep an eye out for group members who might be tempted to "attack" folks they disagree with or try to "fix" those having struggles. These kinds of behaviors can derail a group's momentum, so they need to be steered in a different direction. Model active listening and encourage everyone in your group to do the same. This will make your group time a safe space and create a positive community.

The group discussion leads to a closing time of individual reflection and prayer. Encourage the group participants to take a few moments to review what they've learned during the session and write down their thoughts to the "Respond" section. This will help them cement the big ideas in their minds as you close the session. Conclude by having the participants break into smaller groups of two to three people to pray for one another.

Thank you again for taking the time to lead your group. You are making a difference in the lives of your group members as they seek to *take back their lives*.

Also available from Levi Lusko

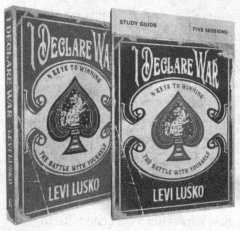

Book
9780785220862

Study Guide
9780310094876

DVD with Free Streaming Access
9780310094913

Whether you recognize it or not, you're at war with yourself. There's anxiety. Selfishness. Self-sabotaging tendencies. But all is not lost. You can win . . . if you choose to engage.

In this five-session video Bible study, Levi Lusko shows how you can fight this battle by declaring war on your thoughts, your words, and your actions. Levi candidly shares about his own struggles to show how you—with the help of the Holy Spirit—can achieve victory by learning to *think right so you can live right.*

Available now at your favorite bookstore,
or streaming video on StudyGateway.com.

New from Jennie Lusko

Book	Study Guide	DVD with Free Streaming Access
9780785232148	9780310112488	9780310112501

Just like some plants need darkness to grow, many of us grow stronger in our faith in the dark and difficult times. It is in the sacred space of pain and promise that we begin to flourish.

In this six-session video Bible study, Jennie Lusko offers biblical hope in your struggles through personal and vulnerable examples of God not only helping her survive the darkness but thrive in it. Fighting and flourishing are meant to blend together, wherever you are.

Available now at your favorite bookstore,
or streaming video on StudyGateway.com.

ALSO AVAILABLE FROM LEVI LUSKO

Win the war against the version of yourself
that you don't want to be anymore.

Now available wherever books and ebooks are sold.

For more information visit LeviLusko.com.